TEACHING BETWEEN THE LINES: HOW YOUTH DEVELOPMENT ORGANIZATIONS REVEAL THE HIDDEN CURRICULUM

TEACHING BETWEEN THE LINES:

HOW YOUTH DEVELOPMENT
ORGANIZATIONS REVEAL THE
HIDDEN CURRICULUM

ANDREW MAGUIRE

NEW DEGREE PRESS
COPYRIGHT © 2021 ANDREW MAGUIRE
All rights reserved.

TEACHING BETWEEN THE LINES:
How Youth Development Organizations Reveal the Hidden Curriculum

ISBN	978-1-63676-379-8	*Paperback*
	978-1-63676-455-9	*Kindle Ebook*
	978-1-63676-380-4	*Ebook*

For Mum and Dad.

Contents

INTRODUCTION		9
PART 1.		**21**
CHAPTER 1.	IN SEARCH OF A COLLEGE MANUAL	23
CHAPTER 2.	THE ORIGINS AND APPROACHES OF YOUTH DEVELOPMENT ORGANIZATIONS	39
PART 2.		**51**
CHAPTER 3.	SHAPING COLLEGE-GOING COMMUNITIES	53
CHAPTER 4.	THE OBSTACLE COURSE OF COLLEGE ADMISSIONS	63
CHAPTER 5.	SUBTLETIES OF THE COLLEGE ACADEMIC CODE	79
CHAPTER 6.	SOCIAL CODES OF COLLEGE	91
CHAPTER 7.	THE POWER OF SELF-EFFICACY	105
PART 3.		**121**
CHAPTER 8.	FROM NAVIGATION…	123
CHAPTER 9.	…TO TRANSFORMATION	135
CHAPTER 10.	PEDAGOGY MATTERS	143

CHAPTER 11. FROM BOOTSTRAPS TO TIGHTROPES:
           INFLUENTIAL NARRATIVES   155
CHAPTER 12. LANGUAGE AS BARRIER AND STRENGTH   169
CHAPTER 13. FACING THE "IN-OUR-FACE CHALLENGES"   181

CONCLUSION   195
EPILOGUE   199

ACKNOWLEDGEMENTS   203
ANNEX   208
BIBLIOGRAPHY   211

Introduction

On a crisp Saturday morning, a group of middle schoolers from across the city descend on the University of Chicago Lab School. These preteens, largely students of color, rub the sleep out of their eyes as they gather for a morning of supplemental coursework. Gifted and motivated to excel academically, each student spends every Saturday and most of their summers throughout middle school at the site. They commit all this time for a shot at breaking into one of the city's most prestigious high schools.

These students are incredible and their futures bright. During these sessions, teachers build students' academic skills, going above and beyond their home high schools. But the students learn much more than additional academic skills. They are introduced to norms that guide the cultures of competitive high schools and prestigious universities. Teachers encourage the students to participate actively, ask questions, and draw on their own personal experiences to understand classroom content. Students are expected to seek out their teachers and counselors for additional help. Amid the shiny classrooms of one of Chicago's most well-funded schools, they begin to learn what immense wealth looks like. In other words, students are learning the *hidden curriculum*—the collection of unstated but powerful codes, norms, and expectations that prove powerful and unfairly influential.

The scene above describes a typical weekend at High Jump, a youth development organization that offers a two-year enrichment program to outstanding middle school students from predominantly low-income, families of color. High Jump is one example of the many dynamic youth development organizations, or YDOs, that support students across the country. YDOs help to unlock greater academic and professional opportunities that students might not otherwise have available to them.

FILLING A GAP

These organizations exist as a symptom of a broken public education system. Each attempt to bridge the opportunity gap carved out by a system that is failing certain kids and certain communities. Let's imagine a young Black student navigating this unfair system. According to sociologist Dr. Chandra Waring, her school will receive less resources and her teachers will discipline her and other students of color more harshly than white peers. If she succeeds academically despite these barriers, she will find little guidance regarding college admission. According to the youth organization The Opportunity Network, "For every one high school counselor, there are nearly 500 students they are expected to support, resulting in a mere thirty-eight minutes of college and career guidance for each student."

If she does get into college, she will have a much harder time completing her degree than her peers. According to writer Matt Barnum, "While two-thirds of white students who start college finish a degree in [six years], only about 40 percent of black students and 50 percent of Hispanic students do. Students from more affluent families are also much more likely to earn a degree than students from low-income families." When she finds a subject area she loves in college and dreams of becoming a professor, she will face a serious uphill battle. According to the National Science Foundation, of US citizens who received doctorates in 2017—an essential component of becoming an academic—only 6.7 percent were Black and 7.1 percent were Hispanic.

On top of deep racial bias in education, there is also a strong class imbalance, particularly in higher education. In a survey of student socioeconomic status across the top ranked 193 colleges in the US, Dr. Anthony Jack cites that "children from well-to-do families, as measured in terms of earnings, took up two-thirds of the seats at the best schools." (The Privileged Poor, pg 4) Similarly, he draws on economist Raj Chetty's work, which found that "students from families in the top one percent—those with incomes of more than $630,000 a year—are seventy-seven times more likely to attend an Ivy League college than are students from families that make $30,000 or less a year." (pg 5) Jack shares an equally sobering statistic, also from Chetty: "The percentage of students from families in the top 0.1 percent who attended elite universities (40 percent) was the same as the percentage of students from poor families who attended any college at all, either two-year or four-year." (pg 5) These statistics bowled me over. Yet as someone saddled with student loan debt despite generous financial aid packages for both my undergraduate and graduate education, I also instinctively know this to be true.

These studies detail barriers of access and achievement. YDOs like High Jump have worked diligently since the 1960s to address these barriers head-on. Though they are not changing the formal education system from within, these groups are offering their students a chance of succeeding like their largely white, wealthy peers.

THE POWER OF THE HIDDEN CURRICULUM
What the overwhelming statistics of educational inequality do not describe, though, are the powerfully embedded norms, language, and expectations that exacerbate this inequality. The hidden curriculum does so by rewarding a particular kind of approach to one's education and socialization, one grounded in being proactive, vocal, and treating relationships as a critical currency. The hidden curriculum has for so long remained unacknowledged, with many privileged students sailing along. They can do so because these norms are built around their cultural upbringing, one of wealth, privilege, and, usually, whiteness.

At many points in your life, you've likely been told that something "is just the way it is," that you have to learn how to "play the game." The hidden curriculum contains "the rules of the game" in school. Educational institutions, and especially elite colleges, are rife with these rules. They include expectations of how to carry yourself in class, engage with teachers, hustle for professional opportunities, and take advantage of the resources that are assumed obvious to you. The rules are also social. They cover how you might talk about your family, your social status, and your future, all signals of your belonging in this exclusive space. Students can be prepared to engage along these rules or be stunned by their presence. The extent of how prepared one feels has a great deal to do with the school and community you grew up in. But as established above, students of color and students from low-income families can't count on their schools to deliver a quality education, let alone model the ways they might need to prepare for college.

Gradually, colleges and high schools are beginning to acknowledge the role of the hidden curriculum. They recognize that for some students, their high schools, parents, and communities match and model the cultures of college campuses, both academically and socially. Often, these students are raised in, or at least exposed to, wealthy, suburban, largely white spaces. But for so many other students, namely those from lower-resourced schools, they cannot rely on the same cultural alignment.

A school's acknowledgement of this problem isn't enough to neutralize the power of this unspoken force. It requires action, to make educational experiences more accessible and eventually weaken the hidden curriculum's force. Who can best bridge the gap brought on by the hidden curriculum? I believe youth development organizations around the country play a game-changing role in this regard.

THE ROLE OF YOUTH DEVELOPMENT ORGANIZATIONS
YDOs are so powerful because they can best facilitate the two steps needed to weaken the hidden curriculum's influence: 1)

by making the hidden curriculum explicit and 2) by reshaping collegiate norms to be more inclusive.

This first step—making the hidden curriculum explicit—is baked into the mission of so many of the YDOs I feature in this book, and many more around the country. They operate with an understanding that the education system is broken and will take great effort and time to fix. These organizations choose to operate from outside the system to support students' educational journeys. YDOs offer community for students who might feel marginalized in their home schools. In their YDOs, young people feel seen, surrounded by peers of similar motivations and backgrounds. YDOs employ varied tactics to not only prepare students with the academic skills they need to succeed in the classroom, but also introduce and translate the subtle dimensions of education, and, in particular, elite universities. Simply put, YDOs are decoders of the hidden curriculum. As I'll detail in the chapters ahead, all of these dynamics best position YDOs to help striving, first-generation and low-income students understand the hidden curriculum in order to navigate, and hopefully transform, educational institutions.

The second step—reshaping college norms to be more inclusive—proves to be a murkier goal for YDOs, but one that is an essential and potentially transformative role that YDOs can play. As trusted partners for students, YDOs can, and in some cases already have, equipped students with the skillset to insist on transformative change themselves. So many of the young people I spoke with were eager to speak out for more inclusive classrooms and institutions, and in fact, many already had. In a world where so much burden is placed on the individual student to adapt, YDOs have an opportunity to use their own voice in this battle. As essential educators, YDO leaders can insist that the system become more inclusive and strive for more equitable educational outcomes. Their willingness to do so and the constraints they face in making those decisions prove the most interesting and complicated part of this analysis as the coming chapters will reveal.

MY JOURNEY

I am drawn to this topic largely from my experience as a first-generation American who ran into parts of the hidden curriculum in my own journey. The stories I heard from first-generation students kept grazing my own high school and college experience. These young folks were not squarely describing my story, in part due to my many privileges as a white man, but elements resonated with me. Depending on how narrowly you define the term "first-generation student" (and there is great debate), you might consider me one. My mom left school at sixteen after earning a high school diploma, while my dad continued on to a PhD in Chemistry. He did so in Scotland though, where both of my parents are from. Though our countries speak the same language, the American educational approach was often lost in translation.

As immigrants, my parents were constantly adjusting to American norms and culture, even though they already spoke the language. They were willing to endure the prevalent guns, Pizza Huts, giant Cadillacs, and frosty winters because they were unabashedly chasing the elusive American Dream. My dad would constantly scheme up his next business idea, an early adopter of the now common side hustle. I often admired the side hustles, no matter how crazy the concept (buying a dental lab, melding a Saab and a Mercedes into a single car, concocting an original line of citrus vodka, and creating pickled orchids for jewelry displays). Our family's path was a classic immigrant tale, hustling hard for a big break. But we weren't necessarily building the kind of capital that unlocked doors in America's most privileged circles, in part because we'd never seen it before.

That changed in January 2006, when my family abruptly moved in the middle of my sophomore year of high school from central Florida to the wealthy Boston suburb of Newton, Massachusetts. That move hugely benefited me, in part by introducing me to the inner workings of privileged, highly educated life in America. My life in one of the country's wealthiest, most competitive suburbs with some of the best public schooling around not only made me a better thinker—it modeled the kinds of lengths privileged families would take to maintain that position for their kids. Test prep courses, private college counselors, paid community service trips abroad, and bankrolling early decision commitments were all common tools of these wealthy families. Just knowing that you could commit to a school months ahead of others, let alone having the financial means to do so, gave them a leg up. Though these advantages were ones that I largely couldn't afford, even knowing about them began to open doors. The power we didn't even fully understand you could wield was suddenly everywhere. My parents' endless chase had finally landed them where the search for the American Dream almost always does: in a dream deferred—to me.

As a teenager, I didn't necessarily aspire to have the level of wealth of my peers, but I did want an impactful path to my future. I could sense their clout was something I might need in order to do that. To effectively navigate this new environment, I started to play by the rules of the privileged game. This happened both intentionally, by preparing aggressively for standardized tests and doggedly pursuing honors courses, and passively, absorbing the language and perspectives of my peers. I began to gain a vocabulary around college admissions. The list of "worthy" colleges expanded well beyond the Ivy League institutions I dreamed of (despite my many years trying to follow in Rory Gilmore's Yale footsteps). I became more comfortable in this wealthy bubble and with it, more confident that I could aim high and not flounder.

Though I couldn't have named it as such at the time, I was building the academic and cultural capital that was ideally preparing me for a smoother college experience. As I transitioned to Vanderbilt University on a generous need-based financial aid package, I felt I could start on more of a level playing field, capitalizing on the abundant resources I (or rather, my financial aid) was paying for. That's not to say there weren't surprises. I still found myself stunned by the extreme wealth of some of my peers, of their ability to so casually enjoy lavish nights out and elaborate spring break trips. I felt unsure of the processes of getting an internship and building professional credibility; I couldn't even sort out how to pick a career path in the first place. At each stage of my adult life, I've picked up on the prevailing norms of "elite" circles and, even if belatedly, tried to catch up so I might also benefit.

LOOKING AHEAD

But as a cisgender, native-English speaking, white man, I am immensely privileged and undoubtedly lucky. If the process of understanding and navigating the subtleties of the hidden curriculum was difficult for me with all my privilege, then how daunting must it be for so many other young folks?

To understand how they do this, I'll first explore in Part 1 what the hidden curriculum is and how it is entangled with America's unequal education system. From there, I'll dive into specific elements of the hidden curriculum and review how YDOs use different approaches to tackle these topics. The chapters in Part 2 consider how YDOs cultivate college-bound cultures, support students in navigating the college application process, prepare them for college classrooms, and build their ability to navigate the cultural and social norms on campus. Through these chapters, I hope to make clear the significant impact YDOs have on young people already. Importantly, Part 2 should recognize the often-overlooked responsibility YDOs have in unmasking the hidden curriculum.

In Part 3, I'll dig into the dynamics that YDOs operate within and the challenging choices they must make. In particular, I highlight the differences in navigational and transformational approaches and how those two approaches show up in pedagogy, language, and narratives. I'll conclude considering the systemic potential of YDOs as a collective. I hope these chapters are viewed not as a critique of the important work of YDOs, but rather a call to consider how each YDO and the sector as a whole can maximize the impact on students. Together, they should help us understand the ways in which both individuals can adjust to the system, but most importantly, how the system could become more inclusive, particularly if YDOs leverage their position to do so.

I'll illustrate the work and dynamics detailed above by highlighting a handful of diverse and dynamic YDOs working across the country. We'll hear directly from administrators themselves, as well as from YDO alumni who can speak to how these programs influenced their trajectories. This book will take you from the classroom of a weekend enrichment program in Chicago to family dinners and college workshops at a community organization in San Diego. We'll travel from the cut-throat climate at elite high schools to the intimate partnerships between new college students and their peer mentors. Throughout, I will let the expertise and lived experiences of those I spoke with lead my exploration and reflection.

In adopting this structure, I aim to reach a wide audience who are directly impacted by the hidden curriculum and by those who have an opportunity to make it less hidden and less powerful. Of course, the intersection of those two groups are those students and administrators participating in YDOs, confronting the hidden curriculum on a daily basis. I hope this book tells their story, one that's often overlooked. Beyond them, I hope to reach other educators and policy makers, whether operating at a community organization, school or governmental body. Although I have adopted a journalistic stance, I am a student of community organizing and policy; I cannot help but want to orient towards potential steps to make educational opportunity more equal.

In doing so, I want to confront the idea that we all *must* learn to "play the game." In the spirit of transformational change,

I hope to shift the dialogue towards how we ensure all young people are not only invited to play the game but are placed in a position to change the game, to redefine it for all players involved. I got tired of hearing "that's just the way it is" as a kid and I'm increasingly tired of hearing it as an adult. I hope this book contributes to the greater team fighting for the new, fairer game.

PART 1

Just as students arriving at college need an orientation to the many components of college life, I believe readers need an orientation to the hidden curriculum and the work of youth development organizations. The next two chapters offer a foundation for all readers to build upon throughout the rest of the book. I'll detail the power of cultural capital and how it influences the hidden curriculum and use language as an example to understand how these dynamics are at play. I'll also provide an overview of the youth development field and offer some helpful categories to differentiate across different YDO approaches. Much like a college orientation, these chapters will only the scratch the surface, but I hope they'll get us all headed in the right direction and ready to learn together.

CHAPTER 1:

In Search of a College Manual

On the first day of class, your professor hands out the syllabus. She walks through the details— the schedule of classes, topics, readings, and assignments. But after just five minutes breezing through the syllabus, she dives right into her first lecture. You look around, but most others seem calm. "Is my copy missing pages of the syllabus?" you think; you're looking for not just *what* you'll do in class, but *how* you should go about doing it. As you work through your first week of classes at your new college, you realize the professor's syllabus offers more explicit guidance than you might find elsewhere. From dorms and dining halls to student club meetings, you wonder how so many of your classmates appear comfortable, as if being a college student runs in their blood.

For many underrepresented students, college orientation is disorienting. While their peers who attended prestigious high schools can more comfortably engage in their college environment, many students will be unfamiliar with college cultures.

Feeling afloat and intimidated, these same students will yearn for clearer guidance. But as sociologist Dr. Anthony Jack puts it, "No manual of 'do's and dont's' or 'when's and how's' circulates during freshman orientation at elite colleges."

These do's and dont's, when's and how's make up much of the hidden curriculum. But why is this curriculum visible for some and hidden for others? Much of it comes down to cultural capital. <u>Cultural capital is</u> "the accumulation of knowledge, behaviors, and skills that a person can tap into to demonstrate one's cultural competence and social status." (Cole, 2019) Interwoven with our wealth (economic capital) and relationships (social capital), our cultural capital proves powerful, particularly in institutions built on it. (Bourdieu, 1975) Universities exemplify this, as they are built around a very narrow profile of cultural capital. Cultural capital manifests in several ways, which accumulate to inform how students experience college cultures.

CULTURAL CAPITAL YOU CAN SEE (& EAT)

Our first impressions provide a surprising amount of information about a person's social capital; physical belongings are a clear indication of cultural capital in a material state. From the books you read to the car you drive, your stuff is often reflective of your economic status and the cultural capital you carry. Students at elite universities make this distinction powerfully clear. The playground of wealthy offspring, elite colleges can be startling examples of the trappings of wealth.

Those sensations of intimidating wealth showed up in my college experience, but I had at least been mildly conditioned to wealth after a few years of high school in the wealthy suburb of Newton, MA. I befriended kids with multi-story homes boasting million-dollar price tags. (Every year, the local newspaper publishes the home values of every single home in town, allowing you to compare price points of all of your classmates' homes. It remains the most apt representation of Newton's cutthroat status war). Perhaps true of most high schoolers, I was finely attuned to material status symbols. In a sea of UGG Boots, North Face jackets, and Starbucks lattes in hand, I felt out of place in my TJ Maxx sale rack coat. I remember the thrill of receiving a hand-me-down sleek black Lacoste polo, which would normally retail at over $100. I felt the power of wearing such a status symbol, even if it was missing a button.

Clothing proves a powerful chasm between university students of different socio-economic backgrounds. Numerous students featured in Dr. Jack's book *The Privileged Poor* reference the proliferation of Canada Goose jackets on campus. The next iteration of what in my college days was the esteemed North Face jacket, the Canada Goose jacket is an overt signal of one's wealth. Their thousand-dollar price tags may as well replace the logo. The effects of their ubiquity are immediate. One student I spoke with, Andrew, a first generation, low-income student at the University of Pennsylvania coyly wondered, "Do I really belong in this sea of geese?" Though he was being tongue-in-cheek, it does reflect the reality that cultural capital alignment influences belonging on college campuses.

When peers with different cultural capital mix, their mismatched norms and expectations breed conflict. I distinctly remember one meal with high school buddies. I strategically scoured The Cheesecake Factory's (notoriously dense) menu to find something under ten dollars, while my wealthier friends ordered themselves a salad, entrée, and, of course, some cheesecake for dessert. When the time arrived to pay, I gave my ten dollars and a few extra bucks for tip and tax, much to the chagrin of my friends. "Let's just split the bill, Andrew," they retorted, scoffing that I'd want to make the payment calculations more complicated by paying specifically by our orders. This continued to be a point of contention for years, with my wealthier friends not understanding how much cost-consciousness dictated my behaviors and decisions. With more financial stability today, I can appreciate the sentiment, the generosity, and trust you signal by agreeing to pay more than your due with the faith others will return the favor in the future. But as a cash-strapped teenager, I felt frustrated by my friends' blindness to my very real constraints.

These memories all rushed back to me as I read Dr. Jack's profile of William, a white student who attended public school before attending an elite university. In Dr. Jack's book, William is considered "Doubly Disadvantaged," a student from a low-income community with a school that didn't model a collegiate culture. This contrasts with the "Privileged Poor," those low-income students who were able to attend elite high schools that modeled and discussed college norms.

Food frequently made William feel marginalized at his university. He explains that for his wealthier peers, eating out was a weekly or even daily experience. "They say, 'I hate going to the cafeteria for lunch. I went to town and got a lobster; cannot believe it's only $30. Home it was like $80 to get lobsters. It's so cheap here.'" You can feel his eyes roll as he says this. I know mine did. He quickly notes, "I cannot eat anywhere else because my meal plan is paid for and that is amazing. To not eat basically free food is ridiculous sounding to me. All you have to do is walk there. Why would I pay for food?" (pg 46)

William is confronting the very different values and norms that he and his peers carry. While his peers place value in the luxury of lobster dinners, he values resourcefulness. Having to confront these misaligned values, and then having to explain your perceived divergence from the "norm" proves an unexpected element of college. In other words, it is a powerful part of the hidden curriculum.

PREVAILING NORMS
While the cultural capital that's visible to students can feel daunting, cultural capital also manifests in subtler, normative ways, which can prove much more challenging. This type of cultural capital can range from the manners we learn and the values we live by to the norms we adhere to. This cultural capital is taught and reinforced through socialization and education. We pick up on what's seen as having cultural value throughout our lives.

Academic and social norms on college campuses narrowly define what it means to be a successful student. As Dr. Jack describes in his book, "Those students who are not familiar with the unwritten rules are unaware of what they are being asked to do—unaware that a crucial part of college is more than mastering the material that they encounter in the classroom...some students discover, to their great consternation, that they are also responsible for deciphering a hidden curriculum that tests not just their intellectual chops but their ability to navigate the social world of an elite academic institution, where the rewards of such mastery are often larger and more durable than those that come from acing an exam." (pg 86)

For instance, university faculty largely expect that students will approach their academic career proactively. This doesn't mean that students must doggedly perform the best in their academic outputs, though that's of course welcome. What faculty expect is that students will proactively seek them out as individuals, mentors, and supporters.

The expectations around being proactive closely track two other influential norms: building relationships and asking for help. Faculty and other academic leaders want to position themselves as resources. Faculty make themselves available for counseling and individualized support during office hours (more on that confusing concept in Chapter 5). They readily offer career advice to students who want to pursue a similar path. And importantly, faculty want to connect students with academic resources when they are struggling with course content.

All of these beneficial resources and relationships depend on a student understanding that they are not only allowed, but encouraged to seek out that kind of support. As Dr. Jack describes in his book, and I heard affirmed in my interviews with first-generation students, this isn't obvious or ever explained. Those students who understand these concepts have seen them modeled in their high schools, which are intentionally trying to mimic college norms, or by their families, who have shared their own experiences in college.

I'm particularly interested in these dynamics because I still struggle to see through them. As an undergrad who had depended so heavily on academic performance to get ahead, I felt allergic to the idea that relationship-building could prove just as powerful. And despite coming to realize so many of these dynamics, I still found myself falling into the same habits when I returned to graduate school a few years later.

THE "RIGHT" WAY TO SPEAK

While the norms above inform how many students and faculty behave in school, there is another powerful way of signaling one's cultural capital alignment: language. Language is deeply linked to one's identity, from the smallest dialectal differences to speaking completely different languages than the one dominating the spaces you occupy. The way language is taught, judged, and reinforced has enormous ramifications on educational opportunity and equity.

In American classrooms, students are taught to learn and use "standard" English, one which is grounded in white speech patterns and no dialects. As the norm established by educational institutions and workplaces, the dominant "standard" English strain implies any variations are non-standard, and therefore wrong. Sociolinguist Dr. Walt Wolfram states it simply: "If people belong to a socially oppressed group, they can count on having their language stigmatized; if they belong to a prestigious group, their language will carry prestige value." (2000)

Educators have been grappling with this dynamic for decades, through their students' biases and their own. "People's intelligence, capability and character are often judged on the basis of a sentence, a few phrases or even a single word." Wolfram explains, "Studies show that children as young as three to five years of age show strong preferences—and prejudices—based on dialect variations among speakers. Teachers sometimes classify students' speech as 'deficient' when it is simply different from the testing norm." (2000) The way students understand the value and appropriateness of their native dialect or language has enormous consequences on their sense of self and educational engagements. Teachers assign and signal those values.

With this in mind, some educators, including Wolfram, have worked to make classrooms more welcoming to linguistic diversity. The most notable flashpoint of this work arrived in Oakland public schools in 1989 when some teachers sought to affirm Black students speaking African American Vernacular English (AAVE) in the classroom. Some teachers in Oakland decided to work against what Wolfram described to me as a common misconception that AAVE is "basically a collection of errors." To counter this, these teachers want to acknowledge the grammatical rules AAVE followed, teaching students how to harness the power of their dialect in parallel with learning standard English. The so-called "Ebonics controversy" became national news, a warped story that suggested these teachers were teaching students how to speak AAVE. Although the Oakland school district relented and removed that portion of the curriculum, the controversy opened the door for continued educational action around linguistic diversity. (*You're Wrong About*, 2019)

Wolfram exemplifies these efforts. For one, he and his colleagues designed a linguistic diversity series that is now embedded in statewide middle school history lessons across North Carolina. The state boasts some of the highest linguistic diversity nationwide, so there are many audiences the lessons resonate with. Through Wolfram's lessons, students learn about the structures and patterns of different dialects and reflect on their own beliefs and biases about language; students, especially students with minority dialects, respond positively to these classes. As Wolfram writes, "Students noted that 'dialects aren't sloppy versions of Standard English'... They came to understand 'there are tons of stereotypes, which are almost always wrong' and that 'dialects represent people's culture and past.'" Teachers, too, see a difference. Wolfram shared a testimonial from one teacher, who noted that "the examination of dialect differences 'has proven to be empowering for my minority students. For many of them, this is the first time they have been told in a school setting that their dialect is valid and not broken.'" (2013)

Language variation is an important part of inclusivity because it is a subtle but powerful dynamic in the classroom. The ways that teachers and students from majority identities might discriminate, intentionally or not, against minority dialectical students cannot be ignored. And yet it often is buried beneath the surface as part of the hidden curriculum.

CODE-SWITCHING AS HIDDEN CURRICULUM RESPONSE
Even in progressive classrooms with openness for linguistic diversity, there is still an assumption that young people will

be better equipped to navigate through elite universities and prestigious future careers if they learn "standard" English. For students where that isn't the prevailing norm in their homes and, in some cases, schools, the expectation is that they'll need to learn to speak "standard" English and know when to switch into it.

Code-switching is the ability to toggle between different languages or dialects. As Jalen Sherald puts it, "Code-switching is the holistic process of assessing a situation and presenting ourselves in the way that we deem most appropriate for the given context. This extends from spoken language to body language, tone, and gestures." (2018)

While code-switching shows up in almost every setting, in educational settings, I understand it in part as students' response to the hidden curriculum. Students pick up on the implication that standard English is the accepted way of speaking, the language required to get ahead in powerful spaces. "The goal of code-switching is to fit into a certain context," explains Dr. Myles Durkee, a psychologist studying the implications of code-switching. Code-switching plays into our fundamental drive to belong in the spaces we occupy and follow subtle social norms in seeking and maintaining that belonging. To navigate these spaces, many students build their code-switching skills (and let's be clear: it is a skill) in order to fit in.

In researching code-switching, I realized that one base assumption often goes unsaid: the term hinges on the idea that communities have a shared code, of language, behaviors, and norms that serve as their connective tissue. If you are aware of this code and can use it appropriately, you signal familiarity and a common playing field with those you're engaging with. But in America, the decision to code-switch and the frequency and degree to which it is done is hugely influenced by one's identity.

For some, our identity allows us to limit our code-switching, either because our identities are in the majority or because they can be invisible. For others, our identities are worn on our skin, in our wardrobe or customs, and cannot be masked. Examples of code-switching show up all the time. For instance, as a queer man at a drag show with queer friends, I might feel comfortable sounding and acting in a way that's perceived as traditionally "feminine." In contrast, if I'm in a space that's viewed as traditionally male and straight-dominated, like a sports bar, I'm likely to switch into a more butch presentation (though let's be real, I'm not fooling anyone). There are more serious and trying examples. A female manager in a male-dominated engineering team might employ traditionally male tactics to compete professionally. In the classroom, students who speak a different language or dialect at home might feel pressured to mask their native way of speaking for one that's deemed more "academic."

Code-switching is far-reaching. This breadth speaks to its benefits, but also masks its many consequences. "Code-switching isn't always a win-win," Durkee cautions. "It's only a win if you do it effectively." To do so, a code-switcher needs to have enough exposure to the other group's culture and the codes implicit in them. For those who can master the skill, there are upsides. As Durkee explains, people with minority identities will code-switch towards more stereotypically majority-held traits because "there's many benefits associated with being perceived as a member of the in-group versus being perceived as a member of the out-group." When applied to the classroom setting, I picture one of Dr. Wolfram's students in North Carolina who feels she has to mask her unique Appalachian dialect and deploy "standard" English to signal to her professor that she should be perceived as a member of the dominant in-group. As a result, she'll hope the faculty is more responsive to her contributions and questions, which may lead to more positive academic outcomes for her.

These benefits perpetuate the practice of code-switching, but that continuation comes with a cost. Durkee explains that "for many individuals who feel forced and pressured to code-switch, it's very taxing because it's a lot of work to have to, one, accomplish your job at a high level, and, at the same time, present a completely different personality." This kind of modulation spans all the norms we've discussed, influencing your mannerisms and how you carry yourself, how you dress, how you speak and ultimately how much effort you put into matching those expectations. As Dr. Durkee simply puts it, "That can be very fatiguing."

CONSEQUENCES OF DIFFERENCES IN CULTURAL CAPITAL

Digging into the dynamics of linguistic diversity and code-switching offers tangible examples of the way cultural capital is embodied. White, wealth-dominated culture has signaled the higher value of particular ways of speaking; this perspective is reinforced through mainstream media and familial interactions, but also powerfully in schools. Teachers and students alike often operate with a preference for the language skills that carry greater cultural capital but do so at the expense of other languages and dialects.

If we apply this same lens to other norms, values, and habits we might have, we can begin to understand which hold value in mainstream culture and which have been marginalized. The hidden curriculum becomes a barrier for those without the "mainstreamed" cultural capita. Students are expected to have it and understand how to navigate it, like how teachers might punish students for using a dialect instead of "standard" English.

Beyond the university setting, the drain of aligning with the dominant cultural capital carries over to professional spaces. Durkee and his peers found that in the workplace, racial minorities will code-switch in order to counter negative stereotypes against their race. However, people with minority identities can also experience stereotype threat, a phenomenon that inhibits performance due to anxieties of being associated with these negative stereotypes (McCluney et. al, 2019). This same phenomenon applies in educational settings. Researchers found that when Black students were primed to think about stereotypes of Black innate intellectual ability, their anxiety about those stereotypes increased and negatively impacted their performance on tests. Similar trends hold for girls who are primed to consider stereotypes of female achievement. (American Psychological Association, 2006)

Colleges have begun to pick up on some of the other consequences of the hidden curriculum and the tensions introduced by these differences in cultural capital. Today, Georgetown University offers a "Mastering the Hidden Curriculum" course. In it, students are introduced to the various manifestations of the hidden curriculum, including many of the above points. The course also reflects on concepts like "impostor syndrome," the sense that they don't belong in this elite institution, that they feel like an imposter when trying to fit in and keep up. (Chatelain, 2018)

Students also pick up on the feeling that a narrow definition of "valuable" cultural capital dismisses the deep value that minority communities carry. The Georgetown course confronts this head-on, a powerful exercise for students who can find affirmation in the face of so much whiteness and wealth.

The benefit of courses like the one at Georgetown is that they allow students to hear the narratives from other first-generation students, which affirm their experiences as common and frustrating. Dr. Marcia Chatelain, who leads the course, hopes it "helps students name the dissonant experience of being away at college while tethered to the challenges of home. In introducing them to this body of academic literature, we are doing more than giving them the vocabulary of sociology or psychology; we are acknowledging the kinds of issues not mentioned in the student handbook."

TAKEAWAYS

Cultural capital is an incredibly influential force in the power dynamics of every institution, and that's certainly true in education. Universities have defined the success of their students around a very narrow type of cultural capital: one that's built around physical manifestations of wealth, but also around the norms common in typically white, wealthy communities. Students are assumed to understand fundamental academic and social norms. Proactiveness, self-advocacy, and a willingness to ask for help prove just as powerful as performing well academically. Students from underrepresented groups often struggle to understand and adjust to these norms. These norms are often reflected and policed through academic language, forcing some students who might not speak "standard" English to code-switch.

In the face of these dynamics, first-generation and other minority students are expected to adopt these norms and to adapt their style, clothes, speech, and behavior. This is the cumulative force of the hidden curriculum. Colleges might think that they're improving access by admitting students of more diverse backgrounds. But in reality, getting in the door is only half the battle. In order to succeed at these institutions, students must confront the hidden curriculum and decide how best to approach it. YDOs help students prepare for this, and in some laudable cases, equip students with the skills to ensure that different forms of cultural capital are valued. The rest of this book explores the unique role of YDOs in teaching, translating, and shaping the hidden curriculum and the challenging dimensions of this work.

CHAPTER 2:

The Origins and Approaches of Youth Development Organizations

---

When you hear the term "youth development organization," what comes to mind? For many of us, we imagine some of the well-established national youth organizations, like the Boys & Girls Club or the Boy Scouts and Girl Scouts. Others may envision sports leagues or arts groups. Some may think of after-school programs and tutoring initiatives. All of these are correct.

The term "youth development organization" is intentionally broad and the sector a true melting pot. "Youth development organizations," or YDOs, focus on developing young people outside of the formal classroom setting. YDOs range from the narrowly academic to those widely focused on personal, social, or creative growth.

As I researched this book, I discovered that the youth development world is an intricately woven and far-reaching web. Each interview I conducted with professionals working in this field revealed a new youth development organization to research. A mapping of just the five largest cities in the US would easily yield dozens of organizations serving different cross sections of their communities. The web of youth development organizations doing powerful work for youth across the country is truly overwhelming, but it's also this breadth of impact that so clearly warrants a spotlight.

ORIGIN STORY

Perhaps the oldest and longest-lasting youth institution is the YMCA, commonly referred to as the "Y." Founded in the UK in 1844 as a Christian fellowship for young men, the institution has undergone numerous transformations in its rich history. In the 20th century, the YMCA blossomed, expanding its reach to a diverse cross section of young people. At its founding, the YMCA focused on public engagement and physical education, but the organization soon grew to embrace a social impact mandate. In 1967, the YMCA in Houston launched the Black Achievers program, an adult volunteer mentoring program that continues today. (A peer program, Latino Achievers, is featured in the coming chapters.) Over the last decade, the Y has continued its community development work, with particular emphasis on health and families. In each of its iterations, the YMCA remained a youth development organization; this speaks to the wide net the category casts.

In contrast to a long-standing organization like the YMCA, the majority of YDOs are young. Of the organizations featured in the book, only two were established before 1989: Sponsors for Educational Opportunity (SEO) and A Better Chance. Both organizations launched in 1963. A Better Chance sought to tap into the burgeoning civil rights movement by supporting talented Black youth, while SEO was built on a model of a wealthy donor creating opportunities for low-income youth. (A Better Chance, 2021) A Better Chance's clear connection to civil rights organizing distinguishes it from the origins of peer organizations. In SEO's case, the founder, Michael Osheowitz, was an investment banker who saw many youths without the same access to opportunities he had. (SEO, 2021) Mr. Osheowitz's story is repeated in YDOs that came later, including one of the most prolific examples of recent years, Year Up. Founded by another Wall Street banker, Gerald Chertavian, in 2000, Year Up is a direct response to Chertavian's frustration that the talented youth he met through Big Brother weren't being supported in their growth. (Year Up, 2021)

Other YDOs were born from the experiences of educators, who grew frustrated with the gaps they continued to see first-hand in the formal education sector. Deborah Bial established the Posse Foundation to try and counter talented students dropping out of college by forming cohorts at particular schools. (Posse, 2021) Christopher Yanov saw students in San Diego being drawn into gangs and other violent situations and launched Reality Changers to offer a safer outlet after school. (Reality Changers, 2021)

THE WHY

The differences in origin stories are notable, but their commonality is even more powerful: each YDO was formed in response to a perceived gap in the formal education system. When formal structures fail certain students, and those structures seem immovable, YDO founders set out to try and bridge the gaps they see. Most YDOs start out with humble goals—aiming to reach a small number of students in a particular community, ensuring deep impact for a small subset of students. For some organizations, these humble roots remain, with a limited scope to a particular city or community. This is the case of Reality Changers, which has grown its reach to over 1,000 students in the city but remained focused on students in San Diego with a particular academic experience. Others, like Posse, have scaled nationally, and even some, such as SEO, expanded globally.

Regardless of scale, these organizations are all established with an understanding that their efforts supplement an education system that fails to deliver quality outcomes for all students. Different metaphors are used to recognize their efforts—as a bridge, a stop gap, even a band-aid. Together, the efforts of the hundreds of YDOs across the country form a patchwork of bridges and band-aids trying to fix a deeply broken system.

YDOs shouldn't have to exist. Their presence is indicative of the injustice of a system that only works best for the few and privileged. I have worked in the social impact sector for a decade. Time and again, I've heard leaders say, "We'll have met our mission when we've worked ourselves out of a job." Just as so many social impact leaders face intractable problems, YDOs are largely founded on the assumption that they'll be necessary in perpetuity, that the system will remain unfixed.

In the face of these overwhelming odds, YDOs are faced with a constant choice of which gaps to bridge and what tactics to take. Unmasking the hidden curriculum is only the first step; the way YDOs empower their students to confront and potentially weaken the hidden curriculum's power, can prove transformative. As I'll unpack in Part 3, YDOs have an incredible opportunity, and a tiresome burden, to reveal the hidden curriculum and change its influence in American colleges and universities.

CATEGORIZING YDOS

Let's apply some structure to this wide-ranging, unwieldy sector. YDOs vary in many ways. First, they vary by scale. Many are hyper-local, serving students in their backyard, while others are regional or national. Some offer a haven for high-performing students in low-performing schools. Others intentionally target poor-performing students in equally poor-performing schools. There are even those serving high performers in some of the best schools, and those that ignore schools all together and reach youth who have left the formal education system.

For the most part, these organizations have evolved with formal education in terms of their pedagogical approach. Educators transitioned from a deficit-model of education to a strengths-based model, highlighting the strengths of students, rather than fixating on filling the gaps in their abilities and knowledge. In recent years, progressive teachers have worked to evolve the strength-based approach to a culturally-relevant or culturally-sustaining model. This approach extends to students' linguistic and cultural differences; teachers began to create classroom activities that allowed students of varying backgrounds to participate in full and be seen as having value. These ideological approaches to youth development map to the varied philosophies of the YDOs featured in the book.

The scale, reach, and diversity of youth development organizations is hard to get a handle on. In exploring the question of the hidden curriculum specifically, though, I began to find common threads in some of the program models. Although they still served diverse geographies and student populations, the organizations I studied fell into three broad categories: academic placement programs, academic enrichment programs, and college prep/skills development programs.

Academic Placement: This first category is often what people think of when they think of organizations that prepare students for college. At a high level, these organizations believe a college degree to be the most impactful intervention they can offer. To do so, these YDOs work to place academically successful students at competitive middle and high schools in order to make them competitive for the most elite colleges. This approach usually requires a great deal of resources, particularly as the organizations provide or negotiate scholarships and other financial support for their students. This model also notably exists at the college level, with organizations like Posse matching talented high schoolers from underrepresented backgrounds to elite universities across the country. However, the organizations I connected with largely focused on earlier education placement opportunities.

When you dig into why these organizations believe in this approach, they reflect a belief that both academic abilities and familiarity with elite educational spaces offer the strongest combination to succeed in similarly elite colleges. For instance, the Oliver Scholars program supports young New Yorkers to be placed into independent schools across the city. Often, this means students are taken from lower-resourced public schools to private and parochial schools flush with funding. Though a challenging transition, graduates of Oliver Scholars consistently enroll in and graduate from college at a much higher rate than peers from their communities. (Oliver Scholars, 2021) In other models, students from middle class communities are similarly supported to level up their educational opportunities. A Better Chance supports primarily families of color in getting students placed in competitive high schools, with a direct track to improved college opportunities. In contrast to many of their peers, their students are often from middle class families and relatively strong public school districts. (A Better Chance, 2021) These two examples serve as a telling reflection of the diversity in the youth development sector, and the academic placement sub-sector specifically.

Although I'll dig into this more in Part 3, these models certainly reflect Dr. Anthony Jack's thesis regarding the value of cultural capital. The students he describes as the Privileged Poor are the very same students benefiting from programs like Oliver Scholars and the more widely known Prep for Prep. These programs seek to help their students to build cultural capital that can be impactful in navigating elite universities. This is especially important for their students, largely first-generation students and students of color, who are more likely to lack that cultural capital due to systemic barriers. By attending a high-quality academic program, students with academic placements in middle and high school also build fundamental academic skills that fast track them in college. In order to achieve these goals, academic placement programs are typically the most expensive model on a per student basis, particularly when either the youth organization or the host educational institution needs to cover the costs of tuition and, in some cases, housing.

Academic Enrichment: In contrast to academic placement organizations, several youth development organizations take the less resource-intensive approach of academic enrichment. These organizations recognize that many students from communities that have low college-going rates need support above and beyond what their schools can provide them. Rather than remove them from the schools and place them in higher performing ones, academic enrichment programs function as a supplement to schools. Think of them as after school time on steroids. SEO is a great example of this model. This program supports public high school students in New York and San Francisco by providing the equivalent of two-and-a-half years of extra English language study and one-and-a-half years of additional math. They do so by asking students to commit three Saturdays a month, five weeks each summer, and multiple weeknights after school for the entirety of their high school tenure. (SEO, 2021)

These programs ask a lot of students, and often of their families, in order to improve their educational opportunities. Like the academic placement organizations, academic enrichment program impact hinges on the idea that these organizations are creating an outlet for highly motivated students to tap into their full potential. That potential often feels overlooked in their elementary and middle schools, but when they turn to programs like SEO, they are affirmed. These programs also intentionally model the kinds of academic norms these students might find at an elite school, which also means they're modeling the academic norms of a college classroom. Like academic placement programs, these academic enrichment programs seek to build both students' academic abilities and their familiarity with the cultures of the universities they're likely to attend. These intensive programs require strong financial investments, but the per student costs are much lower, and so they're often able to operate on a wider scale.

College Prep and Skills Development: The last category of youth development organizations falls into a bit of a catch-all (if this were *Jeopardy*, it would be the Potpourri clues). Unlike the first two categories, these organizations do not provide traditional academic instruction to their participants. Instead, they focus primarily on building tactical skills for students to use in a variety of future settings. Many guide students through the college admissions process. The YMCA Latino Achievers program, for instance, counsels students on everything from writing essays for college applications to completing financial aid applications. (YMCA, 2021) Another organization, Let's Get Ready, started out as a free SAT-prep course before growing to include broader college admissions counseling and peer mentoring. Other organizations focus more broadly on skill building. (Let's Get Ready, 2021) Reality Changers, the San Diego program serving students who are struggling academically, builds academic skills through one-on-one tutoring. This differs from academic enrichment programs in that there is no traditional classroom instruction and content to learn. Rather, Reality Changers mentors provide support on school assignments while also building effective study habits. (Reality Changers, 2021)

These programs are focused on the cultural capital deficit by supporting students through the complicated processes of applying to college and financial aid and on training students a to navigate and succeed in a new academic and social environment. They do this through intensive workshops and mentoring, including with peers or alumni of the program they're in. These programs still ask a lot of their students, but not at the same level of commitment as most academic enrichment programs. In doing so, they can often be more flexible and, in some cases, cast a wider net.

College prep and skills development programs assume that the broader skills development will have a positive halo effect on students' academic development. Together, these improvements position students for future educational and economic outcomes. Notably, these organizations tend to be the most nimble and often operating on smaller budgets. Part of the reason these organizations can exist is because they can reach a wide number of students in a relatively low-cost manner, though the models vary.

TAKEAWAYS

These three categories of youth development organizations offer some structure to a field whose variety reflects both its need and its murkiness. Given that academic support, social support, skills development, and direct advising are all closely related, these categories of YDOS certainly overlap. In almost every example above, the program models draw from fundamentals of other approaches. Almost every academic placement and enrichment program offer supplemental programming on skills development. Many college prep organizations form partnerships with higher education institutions to boost their participants' chance of admission, riffing on the academic placement approach. The blurred lines of this sector speak to the multifaceted barriers in education and the equally multifaceted response the barriers demand.

Ultimately, as YDOs grapple with a dysfunctional education system, they also must fully engage with it to make sure their students can succeed within it. It is at this intersection that the hidden curriculum becomes so meaningful. Understanding the background and varied approaches of these organizations will help us understand the ways in which they teach, translate, and shape the hidden curriculum for their students. As the next few chapters describe, youth development organizations across these categories play an essential role in helping students understand and navigate the hidden curriculum of college. To help readers keep track of the various organizations, I've included an at-a-glance chart of the various YDOs highlighted in the book (see Annex). This tightly woven and wide-reaching web of organizations, with different approaches and touchpoints, improves the odds that the students who need their support, get it.

PART 2

With our foundational course in the fundamentals of the hidden curriculum and the work of YDOs in hand, we can proceed to our upper-level courses on the topic. In the following section, I'll detail the specific ways the hidden curriculum manifests in: college-going communities (Chapter 3), college admissions (Chapter 4), college academics (Chapter 5), and social spaces (Chapter 6). In Chapter 7, I'll illustrate how all of these elements of the hidden curriculum are interwoven, by considering how one powerful trait encouraged in the hidden curriculum shows up.

One critical service YDOs offer is to provide a clearer to-do list for college-bound students. Rise First, a youth-led organization serving first-generation college students, captured this spirit by creating two "roadmaps." The first details the many steps students must take before getting to college. From submitting medical records and financial aid paperwork to enrolling in courses and taking necessary placement exams, the map prompts students to be fully prepared to get started (RiseFirst.org). The second map charts some key milestones through each year of a four-year college experience (RiseFirst.org). It outlines potential expected academic and extracurricular components and carves out lots of space for professional development, an often-overlooked facet of the university experience.

I appreciate that the roadmaps are explicit about small but significant components, such as learning professional email etiquette and proactively socializing with peers in your dorm. The roadmap distills down complex requirements and norms of college experiences, but also encourages first-generation students to stay grounded in their network and lean on loved ones and mentors for support. I hope the coming chapters offer a similar roadmap, one that runs alongside Rise First's maps; in this case making explicit the unstated ways the hidden curriculum shows up at different milestones. When combined with the knowledge of how to make it into and through college, this information can prove empowering for students as they seek to make the most of their college experience.

CHAPTER 3:

Shaping College-Going Communities

Alexa Ramirez was a very social child. So, it's no surprise that as she boarded the bus for a weekend retreat with a bunch of strangers, she immediately started chatting up the girl in the seat behind her. "I remember my first thought was, 'Oh my god, I've never made a friend or talked to somebody who is so open to just talk about the things that we were talking about,'" Alexa shared with me. Little did she know that this young woman, Janice, would become her best friend through high school and college. Alexa and Janice were two of the newest members of High Jump, an academic enrichment program for high-achieving middle school students in Chicago. As they headed out on a three-day retreat with their new peers, all strangers from schools across the city, Alexa was struck by more than her new best friend. She realized, "I'm about to meet people who look like me and who are excited about school and about these topics that I care about."

As Alexa's story begins to illuminate, YDOs create powerful communities by bringing together students with a shared passion for learning and with similar trajectories, family histories, and public-school experiences. This community building plays an essential role in cultivating a college-going culture. Through a communal ethos, YDOs play an important role in ensuring students know college is an option for them, that they understand how it might impact their futures, families, and communities, and help identify the right college for them—academically, socially, and financially.

A SHARED COMMITMENT TO COLLEGE

YDOs unmask some of the hidden facets of the college process that more privileged communities might take for granted. In wealthy school districts, schools can draw out these elements; if they don't, parents who themselves attended college can drive these lessons home (literally). Communities with under-resourced schools and low rates of college attendance cannot do the same as easily. YDOs bridge this important gap and build shared excitement around the college potential for students and their families.

Though the retreat Alexa remembers fondly is no longer part of the program, community building is still integral to High Jump's approach. High Jump's model brings together students of high academic promise from across Chicago for a two-year academic enrichment program. Most students come from low-income families and are students of color and aspiring first-generation college students. Students spend two Saturdays a month and most of their summers in seventh and eighth grade studying. Class time focuses on reading, writing, and math, all with aspirations that students will be competitive for some of Chicago's top charter and private schools.

As High Jump's website explains, their students "share a hunger to learn more, experience more and be more. They also share an uphill climb to fulfill their academic and leadership potential because of limited economic resources." You see echoes of this in Alexa's stories, an eagerness in finding other school-loving kids. That hunger for more, in the face of that "uphill climb," likely helps students stay motivated through weekend classes and extra schoolwork. While no students should have to go those extra lengths to feel fully engaged, in Alexa's case and her High Jump peers, the program offers an energizing outlet.

That shared experience, in the face of obstacles, bonds High Jump students together. Jess Mora, another High Jump alum, echoed Alexa's experience. She also saw the value in being around peers with the shared commitment to learning in the program. Jess was also struck by how comfortable she and her peers were made to feel. This allowed them to take risks and to genuinely explore their interests, including through High Jump clubs on topics ranging from TV and film to French and Spanish languages. One weekend, those interests were on display for a talent show and the otherwise introverted Jess found herself singing Taylor Swift karaoke in front of her whole class. "Looking back, I don't know how they got me to do it; I don't know if I would do that now," Jessica shared. "But it just felt like such a community that it felt like you were just performing in front of your family and that no one was going to judge you for it." This small moment represents how Jess and other students felt supported to learn, grow, and change, but without having to feel "like you have to lose your sense of self, your sense of identity."

While High Jump's convening power makes a positive impact on its students, the organization selects students who are already performing well academically and who likely would have been on the path to college, albeit perhaps a much more difficult path without High Jump's help. Other YDOs, though, must work a lot harder to convince students that college is in their future.

COLLEGE AS A CARROT

The San Diego-based organization Reality Changers contrasts High Jump. Unlike many peer YDOs, which intentionally recruit students with strong academic records, Reality Changers aims for students who struggle academically. Targeting students with lower than a 2.0 GPA, or a C average, Reality Changers creates a supportive extracurricular outlet for academic and life-skills development.

"When you work with students that want to go to college, or at least are aware of it, you can start at a different space than us," explains Jordan Harrison, director of programs at Reality Changers. "On average, our eighth-grade students can only name two universities." The consequences of this very different student population have wide-reaching impacts on the program's design. While college is initially treated "as a far-off carrot," Harrison's team focuses on "how can we have a relationship with you today. I think that informs our program, and how we support the students, how much time and effort goes into building deep relationships, and then providing experiences that make the students want to come back."

With two primary program offerings, College Town for eighth to eleventh graders and the College Apps Academy for twelfth graders, Reality Changers comes across as very college-focused on paper. In practice, the College Town program fundamentals includes after-school tutoring, homework help, and test prep—all conducted in a safe and comfortable student space. To make their services resonate with students, Harrison must go beyond the curriculum to the individual experience of showing up to Reality Changers.

Each night, students come together for a community dinner, offered for free as an essential element of Reality Changers' program. Harrison and his team know you can't just convene a bunch of teenagers and assume all will get along and feel comfortable with one another. With each student, they think through any number of dimensions. "How are we greeting them? Do they have a name tag? Do they have friends that are going to be in the program with them? We're thinking about things that are going to make them want to just show up and make us the hotspot for students to be at," he explains. "Because if we are just talking about college, they probably won't even show up."

This intentional thinking seems to be working. When I spoke to Dagim Aboye, an alum of the program, two words came up on repeat: cool and fun. Whether going to Reality Changers after school to do homework or "grind through college applications," Dagim always felt it was fun. The community clearly had something to do with Dagim's spirited endorsement. "I felt more at home at Reality Changers than I did at my high school because of the diversity. I could relate to almost everyone there because most people are first-gen, immigrant, or low-income, while my high school was predominantly white."

Having alumni with the level of enthusiasm Dagim has for the program doesn't come easily. As Harrison readily notes, Reality Changers has to play a long game. "Sometimes it doesn't even click for maybe one, sometimes two years, before a student really catches on," he shares. "And part of it is just the culture, the community that they're part of. Slowly, you see them making different friends." Harrison draws a direct correlation here between the program's effectiveness and how close students feel to their peers.

At the same time, Harrison is quick to note that creating bonds at Reality Changers should not be at the expense of other relationships. As he explains, "[I]t's not about them ever leaving who they are. So you can still have outside folks that you're cool with. But if you need to go to the library, and they went to the skate park, it's about helping you make some of those smaller, better decisions and having a community that would actually celebrate those decisions." It's this focus on shifting decision making and priority setting that requires the program to focus on students "buying into the community and then believing it, and then we'll design it for college."

ADULT NUDGES, MATURE DECISIONS
When I spoke to many YDO alumni about their introductions to these programs, I kept feeling frustrated at the very adult

decisions they were faced with. I imagine a young Dagim or Alexa having to decide whether they want to commit some of their precious free time to join a YDO. Though they and other alumni shared the fun memories they've had, YDOs still do require an investment of time and energy. Privileged kids generally don't have to make that decision. They can choose to play and count on their schools to deliver a quality education. Their parents might insist they take on extra academic opportunities, tutoring, or after school volunteering. These parents do so not out of a fear that their child won't get a good education, but more that the extra engagements will give their children a leg-up.

Many of the first-generation, low-income, and other marginalized students YDOs serve must try and see the long-term benefits participating in a YDO could offer them. That's not easy foresight to have with the other competing demands of teenage life. These students do usually understand that their future opportunities will be constrained by the broken system they're in. For students at organizations like High Jump and Reality Changers, the decision to invest their time in these programs is in direct response to their schools failing them. Whether by not engaging them enough, like so many High Jump students, or by letting them slip through the cracks, like many Reality Changers students, these students' schools have failed them. YDOs bridge this gap, supporting students' academic achievement and future educational opportunities.

The appeal of a YDO program is much easier to see without adolescent goggles on. It's no surprise that influential adults play a key role in helping students find their way into programs like High Jump and Reality Changers. For Dagim, his mom knew of the program; Reality Changers is well known in his community, so his mom did not hesitate in suggesting he apply. For Jess, her family saw her cousin enter and thrive in High Jump. My interviews with young alumni of YDO programs revealed that many were nudged (or in some cases, forcefully pushed) to apply and attend. Many others will be referred by their own teachers, who recognize that their own schools are failing their students, and that additional support is best outsourced to a YDO.

For Alexa, one of these encouraging teachers started her journey to High Jump, but it proved to be a near miss, twice over. She first learned about the program from a teacher, who handed out fliers to sign up for the program. She remembers all of her classmates throwing the flier away, but she rushed to the High Jump website during computer lab hours. The videos she saw got her even more excited, but her classmates quickly undermined her enthusiasm, telling her it was crazy to volunteer for summer school. She did have a summer camp at her local park that she enjoyed, so with that in mind, she too moved on from the idea.

Weeks later, though, her dad came home, describing a program his coworker had encouraged him to get Alexa into. It turned out to be High Jump and this time, it was Alexa's dad who insisted she apply. Despite her protests, Alexa's dad reminded her of one of his go-to life lessons: "[Y]ou just should never turn down any opportunity until you have it in your hand and then you can actually have the choice to say no." When she did get in, she was still hesitant, and for the first time ever, her dad, normally very encouraging of his daughter's independent decision-making, tipped the scales. As Alexa explained, "[I]t was the only time that he's ever told me that he would be really disappointed in me if I didn't decide to go." It was the perfect moment for her dad's influence, because, as Alexa simply described, High Jump "changed my life."

TAKEAWAYS

This moment in Alexa's life was a clear fork in the road, and her and her family's decision to embark on the High Jump path will likely have a positive ripple effect. It led to her attending one of the most competitive private high schools in Chicago and today thriving at Pomona College. She's maintained that outgoing, bubbly personality, now with streaks of vibrant pink in her hair. She is undoubtedly on track to make a splash in whatever professional field she chooses to enter.

But her success and her family's opportunities potentially hinged on that fork in the road. Alexa and students like her shouldn't be expected to make adult decisions as kids. The fact that they do is a firm indictment of a broken system.

Thankfully, a YDO was there to bridge the gap, as they so often are for young people with great promise but few options. This is not to say High Jump gets the credit for Alexa's hard work and determination, or her family's investments in her growth. But the supplemental opportunities offered from a YDO like High Jump offered Alexa a space for deep learning. She found a best friend and a community of likeminded peers to feed her love of learning. That impact cannot be understated.

CHAPTER 4:

The Obstacle Course of College Admissions

After graduating college, Kathleen Fuchs Hritz worked for six years at the YMCA in Nashville supporting their Latino Achievers program. This after-school program worked primarily with first-generation students from various Spanish speaking countries to navigate the college admissions process and build leadership and life skills. She spent a lot of her time translating for students, but she wasn't translating into Spanish or English. She was translating the college admissions code. Because as Fuchs Hritz would tell her students, "The college process is not in English, and it's certainly not in Spanish; it's really its own language."

Each step of the college admissions pathway is steeped in an unfamiliar language and particular norms that feel completely foreign. This lack of familiarity proves prohibitive to many students, a lasting roadblock that prevents young people from making it into college. Most students and families who make it through the college process for the first time will tell you that it feels as complicated and exhausting as an obstacle course. There are different hurdles, from application deadlines and requirements to financial aid and even short-listing colleges that might be a good fit. College admissions prove as much a test of your ability to run the obstacle course as it is a test of how insightful a thinker or potential future leader you might be. The hidden curriculum is responsible for all these stubborn obstacles, and this is often students and families first time confronting these head-on. YDOs can play a crucial role in easing the process.

DE-STRESSING THE DISTRESSING STANDARDIZED TESTING

In the admissions process, almost everyone's obstacle course race begins with standardized testing. The SATs and ACTs, America's two premier standardized tests, were introduced as a tool for colleges to more uniformly measure academic aptitude. As Paul Tough astutely unpacks in his fantastic book *The Inequality Machine*, these tests no longer serve to gauge just aptitude. Instead, the test results reflect a student's knowledge of strategies to outwit the test. While some savvy students may figure out the approaches on their own, many wealthy students gain these skills through an emergent industry of test preparation tutors.

This industry was easily the most shocking element I discovered when moving to the Boston suburbs as a teenager. I was outraged to find out that families could pay thousands of dollars to send their kids to these test-prep tutors and radically improve their test scores. It seemed like the most egregious influence of wealth on what was ostensibly a meritocratic process, and yet my peers largely shrugged it off. It was seen as an inevitability in their lives that they'd enroll in these very courses, just as it was an inevitability that they would pursue honors classes, captain a varsity sports team, and continue on to an elite university. If it beefed up the college resume, it was going to happen.

Tough illuminates this reality by introducing us to Ned Johnson, president of PrepMatters. As the leader of a test-prep company based in the hyper-competitive DC suburbs, Johnson charges a whopping $400 per hour for his tutoring. Interestingly, his approach is largely a psychological one, rather than a tactical one. Tough explains that the College Board (distributor of the SAT) and the ACT "insist in their public statements that their tests are objective, reliable measures of students' academic ability. And students internalize this idea. They walk into Johnson's office convinced that their score on the test will reveal something significant about them." (Tough, pg 27)

Johnson is decidedly against this notion and reflects this in his work. "Every reference he makes to the tests is dismissive—they're 'stupid' or 'silly' or 'a bunch of malarkey,'" Tough writes. "The tests are not in fact designed to measure how smart you are. They are designed to assess how well you have mastered the tricks of taking standardized tests." (Tough, pg. 28) And with that as his mantra, Johnson introduces these tricks while diminishing how much his students might internalize the pressure of the tests.

Johnson offers numerous strategies including: substituting real numbers to solve algebra questions; treating reading comprehension questions like they're written by lawyers, not poets, to see if there's any small detail to make a mostly right answer wrong; and eyeballing geometry diagrams to estimate the right answer first before considering the available options. His efforts pay off. One of his students, Ben, explained his success under Johnson's guidance. "Once you realize that there are loopholes and backdoors to the test, it loses its value. If you can skirt around what they want you to do and still get the right answer, you realize at that point that they're not really testing skills." (Tough, pg. 102) This is a powerful perspective to have in taking a test that carries so much weight.

When families can buy access to these strategies for their children, it's no surprise that standardized tests reflect serious bias against lower income students. Already accused of racial and cultural biases, the College Board has finally explicitly acknowledged the flaws of their test. In 2013, their new president released data that showed "students' SAT scores tracked their family income in a direct and linear fashion." (Tough, pg. 77) Despite efforts to reform the SAT, including making SAT prep classes freely available through online course platform Khan Academy, standardized testing remains a biased indicator of academic preparedness.

The power of standardized testing may be waning. While some schools have moved to test-optional admissions (notably the University of Chicago and the University of California system), most top-ranked universities continue to require standardized test scores from applicants. This changed when COVID-19 made in-person testing nearly impossible. Since March 2020, hundreds of colleges, including notable holdouts like Harvard and Yale, have shifted to test-optional admissions. (Glass, 2021)

The result: a surge in overall applications. This has also meant more applicants from underrepresented groups, which fortunately seems to be translating into more diversity in admissions offers. Now the true test will be whether students in these historically underrepresented groups are able to afford tuition and housing costs and accept these offers, and once they're in the door, how they'll fare in systems that are often unwelcoming. It also remains to be seen if universities will keep these pandemic provisions around standardized testing in place in the long-term. (Glass, 2021)

Understanding the stark disadvantages that many lower-income, first-generation students have in standardized testing, YDOs have offered standardized testing resources to these students for years. YDOs provide a counterbalance to the unfair practice of paid test prep courses. They do so through intensive and freely available test prep curricula as part of their services. One YDO operating in numerous cities across the US named OneGoal tries to take a very balanced approach in their test prep programming.

OneGoal's three-year program model supports students through the junior and senior year of high school and first year of college. They work within high schools, training teachers to use the OneGoal curriculum to support selected students with a holistic academic, social, and college counseling model. In the junior year, the focus is on boosting students' GPAs and standardized test scores to make them as competitive as possible for college applications.

As Senior Director Nicole Petraglia shares, OneGoal teachers tread carefully in this work as they try to stay grounded in a culturally responsive pedagogical approach. For example, before they dive into the details of test prep, teachers place these tests in context. This includes detailing the tests' racist past and the idea of stereotype threat.[1] Then they acknowledge the reality that colleges weigh test scores heavily in admissions. As Petraglia explains, "[W]e try to give as much information as we can and support fellows through their feelings and how to process all those things, and cache it as 'We're doing this to set you up to have the most choices.'" Petraglia admits it's difficult to strike the balance between sharing the reality of a biased system without completely discouraging students from pushing past these barriers towards brighter outcomes.

THE EXPECTATIONS BEHIND THE PROMPT: COLLEGE ESSAYS

For students who can persevere through the standardized testing process, the next obstacle on the course is completing the applications for specific colleges. An integral element of that process is writing a compelling personal statement. On its surface, these essays might not seem very coded. You're given a prompt and you respond. Buried beneath the prompts, though, are an intricate web of expectations for the

---

[1] Stereotype threat is phenomenon that inhibits performance due to anxieties of being associated with these negative stereotypes. In educational settings, researchers suspect this same threat explains at least some of the gaps in standardized testing for minority students and young women. (American Psychological Association, 2006)

kinds of stories admissions readers want to hear and how to write those stories in a compelling way.

My friend Ali Thomas has advised high schoolers in both the US and globally on their college admissions process, with some common mistakes and some unique cultural differences. Consistently, Thomas read first drafts "riddled with SAT vocab words," with students striving to come across as perfect and mature, rather than presenting a more authentic voice. She'd readily tell students, "[T]his doesn't sound like an 18-year-old" and suggest they write with a more accessible vocabulary.

While some students struggle with stuffy language, others must consider how open to be in their writing. As a college counselor at a charter school outside Boston, Susan Johnson loves working with her seniors to write compelling college essays. She sees it as an opportunity for students to own their narrative and "show [their] humanity" beyond GPAs and SAT scores. Johnson readily acknowledges, though, that the process can be quite stressful and that students often arrive to the process with preconceived notions of these essays. She explains that many students feel like they're expected to "tell the hardest thing that's ever happened to me or feeling like they're not telling a serious enough story." This isn't surprising and frankly, a serious approach is often rewarded.

In his book, Paul Tough features a resilient low-income student, KiKi, as she navigated her admissions process and early days at Princeton. Throughout her childhood, KiKi experienced significant poverty and constant transience, posing serious challenges to her education. Despite this, she remained a straight-A student. As she started applying to colleges, and scholarships in particular, she felt the required essay prompts asked the same thing: "Tell us about a time in your life when you overcame adversity. Tell us the worst thing that ever happened to you." She realized that her tenth-grade year, which she spent squeezed into a single motel room with her six family members, was exactly the narrative readers wanted to hear. As she told the story, she felt sad, angry, and, eventually, cynical. "The whole process began to feel transactional, like she was trading her pain for college admission offers and scholarship dollars," Tough writes. "The worst year of her life had become a commodity." (Tough, pg 148)

KiKi's story is genuinely incredible and does reflect a resilience and commitment to learning that should be rewarded. While tapping into past challenges can be an effective application approach, there's a risk that it breaches into "performative trauma." This is a common trend in admissions processes across institutions, where applicants feel they need to lead with the darkest moments in their lives to prove they're worthy of a spot in that college or fellowship or grad school. This kind of experience can retraumatize young people.

Many students accessing college admissions support from YDOs might feel similarly constrained by the process. Through trusting advisors and a lot of real talk, YDOs are well-positioned to dig into colleges' expectations and how the essay might factor into the dynamics of a student's application. When Lena Eberhart works with students at Let's Get Ready, she often finds that they hold back in their essays, to their detriment. "They were trying to hide the most interesting things about themselves in order to fit what they assumed was the desired profile," she explains.

Eberhart must work intentionally to draw out the stories that make students unique, as these were the stories they could tell authentically. Often, these unique perspectives also captured some of her students' more trying circumstances. In this way, Eberhart saw it as "opportunistic in an empowering way," with students tapping into universities' interest in diverse students while still representing themselves in the way they feel most comfortable.

Her work with students at Let's Get Ready offers a perfect example of how YDOs can help students become aware of the hidden curriculum of college admissions and then help them decide how to respond. Eberhart and her colleagues aren't coming into their conversations insisting students proceed a certain way. Instead, they present the realities of the admissions process, and the ways students might position themselves for acceptance, while acknowledging the taxing dynamics at play.

FAFSA: A FAULTY TOOL

On this metaphorical obstacle course, students might feel they can rest easy and catch their breath after submitting their applications and many essays. Then they turn the corner and suddenly face the daunting task of financial aid applications. Wrought with complicated forms, technical headaches and consequently challenging family dynamics, this process feels like wading through a mud pit, army crawls under barbed wire, and climbing a ten-foot wall. It's slow going, sometimes painful, and intimidating.

I remember that feeling of facing these obstacles and the dread of diving in. From a young age, my family encouraged my aspirations to go to college, but they also made it clear I'd have to score some serious scholarships to cover my costs. Though my dad has a PhD, he completed all his schooling in Scotland, where all of his costs were paid for. So the financial aid process in America was truly foreign to my entire family. We waded in with little knowledge and stumbled through with fingers crossed. That experience is startlingly common.

In her work at the YMCA, Fuchs Hritz focused on helping her Latinx students navigate the numerous technocratic hurdles of the college admissions process. None proved more difficult than the dreaded FAFSA. For those who have applied for financial aid in the US, FAFSA (Free Application for Federal Student Aid) is the required federal form to capture you and your family's financial status and assets. But for a high school senior to navigate complex financial dynamics on a less than user-friendly form is the epitome of absurdity. To this day, Fuchs Hritz finds it complicated; "I'm actually starting an MBA program and then filed the FAFSA. My husband and I both have maste"s degrees and we're like, 'Where do I look for this?' 'What do you mean it compounds continuously?' 'What does that mean?!'"

This only got more complicated for some of Fuchs Hritz's students, particularly for those with undocumented parents. Due to their immigration status, these students would face blocks in the FAFSA system. Fuchs Hritz picked up some particularly niche knowledge in helping students through these situations. If you have an undocumented parent, she advised, "You enter all zeros and you have to hit submit. But it's gonna stick, and it's not gonna let you go forward, you have to hit Submit two or three times and then it lets you go... Isn't that weird, in-depth knowledge that I have? And then at the end, too, you can't submit it online, you have to print that signature page and mail it." The FAFSA is intended to be a simple, one-size-fits-all form. Yet it proves completely unwelcoming for students who should deeply benefit from it. The FAFSA's quirks illuminate how small, technical components can prove powerful barriers to accessing education.

Fuchs Hritz is not alone in lamenting the FAFSA's maddening labyrinth. The Gates Foundation convened numerous stakeholders behind an initiative called Fixing FASFA. This initiative was driven by the fact that every year "as many as two million students who are likely eligible for aid don't even apply." In a helpful explainer video, the Fixing FAFSA team shares that FAFSA applications are longer than annual tax forms. With over one hundred questions to fill out, the FAFSA is riddled with questions that are irrelevant to the overwhelming majority of students. As Jane Hickey, a financial aid advisor from the University of Maryland Baltimore County, put it: "On a good day, it's complicated. On a bad day, it's almost insurmountable for them."

It's estimated that half of high school seniors didn't complete the FAFSA form in 2021 (Form Your Future, 2021). With that level of disengagement, students are collectively forgoing $24 billion a year in financial help. (Johnston, 2019) This is where the picture around admissions during COVID-19 blurs. While students with marginalized identities are being accepted at higher numbers, the financial aid they're offered won't necessarily increase. Students would first need to know that applying for federal financial aid is an option, then become familiar with the FAFSA process, and finally be able to complete the forms, including gathering important family financial information. Even then, colleges might not be able to meet demonstrated financial needs, due to tighter budgets and uncertain financial prospects following the pandemic.

THE MYTHS AND MYSTERIES OF FINANCIAL AID

Like the FAFSA, college financial aid decisions are similarly confounding. Susan Johnson shared that better understanding the provisions and calculations of financial aid proved to be both the best surprise for some students and the worst news for others. For her high-achieving students, Johnson gave them surprisingly good news: the most competitive colleges in America tend to also give the most generous aid packages. Many institutions, particularly those with large endowments, have committed to meet 100 percent of an admitted student's financial need. They do so while still being need-blind, meaning a student's relative ability to pay is unknown when admissions officers assess their application.

The most generous schools commit to offering aid packages with only grants and on-campus jobs called work study, but not loans. My alma matter, Vanderbilt University, is often lauded for making these commitments in recent years (and motivates alumni like me to continue giving to the school). But I remember being shocked at the generous financial aid package I received from Vanderbilt, in part because I knew of its prestige and its corresponding price tag. It's a perplexing and rarely discussed paradox that the more competitive a school is, the stronger their financial aid offerings.

This is incredibly important knowledge, particularly for students with high financial need, but it often goes unsaid for these students. While these students still face an application process that is stacked against them, if accepted, they could benefit from more robust financial aid offers. Many lower-income applicants are intimidated to apply to highly selective colleges in part because they assume that even if they are accepted, they'd never be able to afford it.[2] But that is far from the truth.

On the other end of the spectrum, students who can't compete at the most prestigious universities face a daunting reality. In advising her students who fall into this category, Johnson explains, there are very few options where they can be both a competitive applicant and receive generous financial aid. In many cases, universities will only give eligible students a Pell Grant, a federal grant offered to families in the lowest income brackets. She explained this is completely inadequate; for a family making less than $60,000 a year, the maximum Pell grant is $7,000. This reality can be particularly frustrating for her Black students, who are often interested in attending a Historically Black College or University (HBCUs). While these institutions can provide a fantastic education and a tight-knit community, their endowments tend to be much smaller than many of their predominantly

---

[2] It's worth noting that in recent years, we have seen a shift in colleges giving more aid to wealthier families. As Paul Tough asserts in *The Inequality Machine*, "American colleges collectively now give more institutional aid to each student with a family income over $100,000, on average, than they do to each student with a family income under $20,000." They do so to attract families that are able to pay for most of their students' college costs but would be more likely to send their child to a school offering them aid.

white peer institutions. Johnson lamented, "This is totally an exaggeration, but it feels like you can either get into Williams [College][3] or you go to a community college. It feels like the middle is dropping out."

BUILDING A COLLEGE LIST

All this information is incredibly important when developing a college list in the first place. Unfortunately, many students don't come to understand the financial feasibility of colleges until they've already completed the admissions process. To better anticipate this, mentors and advisors can prove essential to helping students prepare their college lists to align with their personal needs and financial constraints from the start of the admissions process. Particularly for young people whose families do not have the time or knowledge to helpfully advise them, advisors prove to be critically important in just knowing when and where to apply. They can introduce students to concepts like early action and early decision (the option to apply to a school in an early priority cycle that locks in your admission well before other colleges notify).

The results can be powerful. In one Texas program, students who received counseling enrolled 8 percent more frequently than their peers (Barnum, 2021). Unfortunately, advisors like Susan Johnson are hard to find. The advising sector is woefully under-resourced and poorly trained to support those students that need it most. As the Chronicle for Higher Education reports, "School counselors are overworked and

---

3   Williams College is consistently the top-ranked liberal arts college in the US, with a remarkably high endowment and low acceptance rate. (U.S. News and World Report)

underfunded, serving a median of 482 students each, nearly twice the 250-to-1 ratio recommended by the American School Counselor Association." (Friess, 2019)

In these cases, YDOs can fill an important gap. Whether they do so with full-time staff members or peers from students' colleges, YDOs are able to equip students with the knowledge, timelines, and tools necessary to make it to college. An alumna of OneGoal, Ashleigh Stewart, spoke about how much her program director helped her get on a path to college she hadn't ever imagined for herself. He encouraged her to pursue her passion for softball and aim for a scholarship opportunity to play at the collegiate level, which is exactly what she did. As Ashleigh said, "He made me realize my worth." (OneGoal, 2021)

At Let's Get Ready, peer mentors serve as pseudo-counselors, helping students understand some of the common pitfalls of navigating college academics. Monica Duque was part of the program before they added the peer mentorship component. She's since returned as a staff member for the organization because she knows how much she would have benefited from that kind of guidance. As a freshman, Duque enrolled at the University of New Haven and decided to pursue civil engineering because her dad was an electrician and she'd always been good at math and science. But Duque found herself struggling both with the academics and the social dynamics of being in a predominantly white institution. She transferred to the University at Buffalo and found more comfort there. However, she continued to bounce around different majors, and ended up needing to load up on fifty course credits her senior year in order to graduate on time.

Duque's experience was trying and she remains saddled with tens of thousands of dollars of debt. For her, the opportunity to serve as a coach at Let's Get Ready meant she could help students avoid her own struggles. "I don't want kids to have to go through being six figures in debt right out of college," she shared. Her story reflects the important positive influence mentors and counselors can play in helping students navigate which colleges to apply to and how to persevere through them.

TAKEAWAYS

These many examples illuminate the deeply entrenched, often subtle, barriers built into the college admissions process in America. As Anthony Jack wrote in the *New York Times*, "Money talks and privilege walks. In the case of college admissions, it saunters through wrought-iron gates, past signs emblazoned with 'Welcome Class of' and into seats at convocation." If we want to make higher education more accessible and equitable, we have to make the process reflective of that. YDOs often fill this gap, compensating for under-resourced schools, archaic bureaucracy, unfamiliar territory, and a bias toward the wealthy. The college admissions process remains a language that's native to multi-generational students and wealthier, privileged families and completely foreign to most other students, like Fuchs Hritz's students in Nashville. YDOs serve as very necessary interpreters of this deeply coded process. While they cannot necessarily eliminate the many obstacles, they can at least prove an effective training ground to prepare for this grinding process.

CHAPTER 5:

Subtleties of the College Academic Code

David Thai and I met while we were both living in Vietnam on prestigious fellowship programs. By first impressions, I saw someone who had fully mastered the college code, having thrived at an Ivy League institution and graduated with a renowned fellowship. Like so many of us though, his resume papered over (literally) a more nuanced story.

David grew up in a low-income community in inner-city Philadelphia, where his dad provided for the family as a fish monger. He excelled in his high school, taking AP and IB classes, but it was a far cry from the intimate, well-resourced classrooms of his college peers' private schools. David described feeling like he lacked "academic and professional capital" when arriving at the University of Pennsylvania. "I remember sitting in chemistry lab and I thought, wow, we each get our own Bunsen burner. In high school, all 100 of us in our class shared one Bunsen burner but no one could touch it. Everyone crowded around one little table and then the teacher would do the activity." He admits that in some of his college science classes, he fell behind quickly, overwhelmed with material that was treated as review for his peers but brand new to him. When his academic struggles mounted, he didn't feel comfortable seeking out supportive resources. When encouraged to attend professors' office hours, David thought, "I don't want to bother professors." The way he explained his discomfort to me was simple; he "came from a place where asking for help meant being a burden."

David's struggles—keeping up with class content, understanding available resources, navigating new classroom dynamics, building rapport with faculty, asking for help—are hallmarks of the implicit academic code of college. For some students, particularly those from wealthier families and communities, these norms will be more familiar when they enter college, mirroring their high school climate. In contrast, students from underrepresented backgrounds often find these norms surprising, unsettling, and difficult to adjust to. YDOs help a small subset of these students bridge these differences by preparing them for a collegiate academic environment.

FINDING YOUR WAY AROUND A CLASSROOM
In Dr. Anthony Jack's *The Privileged Poor,* he puts forth a powerful paradigm to capture wildly different experiences of college students, especially students from low-income families. Jack mainstreams an often overlooked dynamic: that "over 50 percent of the lower-income black undergraduates who attend elite colleges get there from... well-endowed, highly selective schools that pride themselves on fostering independent thought and extending beyond the classroom

through close contact with faculty." (pg 10) That group, whom he calls the "Privileged Poor," comfortably navigates elite universities, drawing on the familiar experiences and norms of their largely private high schools. In contrast, low-income students who broke into top tier universities from minimally resourced public schools, whom he calls the "Doubly Disadvantaged," endure a steep learning curve of new norms in and out of the classroom.

One major differentiator, Jack argues, is the academic and cultural capital Privileged Poor students build in high school that carries value in elite colleges. These students might be more familiar with classic work in certain fields, understand expectations around faculty-student relationships, and have strategies to engage in classroom discussions that college professors appreciate and reward. They're equipped with study skills, understandings of how to structure essays, research topics, and manage workloads. This capital serves privileged students greatly in college, as they can more smoothly transition into classroom and campus cultures alike. Their high school experiences revealed the hidden curriculum, avoiding the unpleasant surprises in college that the Doubly Disadvantaged face.

There are several academic norms that change from high school to college, many of which high-performing high schools will try to model for students at an earlier stage. The University of Georgia recognized how unfamiliar these new academic environments could be, especially for first generation students. In response, they developed a first-generation student handbook. The guide offers some helpful contrasts between a typical high school and college environment.

One example is visually apparent for students: very different class sizes. Students in most colleges, even at tiny liberal arts colleges, will experience both large lectures with hundreds of students and very intimate seminars with up to a dozen students. With varied sizes, the guide advises, come very different styles of teaching. Some professors may lecture with no visuals, while others will rely heavily on visuals and slides. In some cases, the class will be structured as a lecture, with minimal participation from students. In other classes, professors will expect student contributions to drive most of the conversation, with only opening remarks to orient class discussion. These varying styles also mean that in some cases, professors will recap content covered in readings for the class, while others will assume readings done outside of class establish a baseline understanding for class sessions to build from.

Colleges also offer a fundamentally different daily cadence. Unlike high school, where every minute is planned and schedules are set for you, college students must navigate a great deal of free time and negotiate their own schedules. This also means that students have to manage their workloads accordingly; it's not uncommon for multiple classes to have major due dates on the same days. This rhythm of assignments requires a great deal of time management and positive habit formation.

The main message that the University of Georgia's manual tries to articulate is that students must undergo a fundamental reorientation to their academic experience. Students must move away from a system where others—teachers, parents, counselors—guided their learning and success and instead take that responsibility on themselves. As the manual states,

"Your success depends upon the decisions that you make." My takeaway is a little different. Yes, embracing newfound autonomy is an important part of students' personal development at college. But the burden is not, and cannot entirely be, on students to navigate this totally unfamiliar environment. YDOs offer their students a reminder that one's network is an invaluable resource.

MIDDLE SCHOOL MODELING

College academic environments create a lot of pressure on students, along with all the other social and cultural dynamics they must adjust to (more on that in the next chapter). YDOs recognize this and work intentionally to better prepare students for this transition, easing them in by introducing them to some of these academic norms before they reach college.

The approaches taken by YDOs vary. For academic placement organizations, they work to place students in the schools that model these academic norms firsthand. For academic enrichment and skills development organizations, these are introduced through extracurriculars. High Jump, however, deploys academic enrichment approaches designed to best position their middle school students to break into the top-performing schools in the city. The organization channels both methods of academic placement and enrichment programs to maximize the best outcomes for its students.

A fundamental component of High Jump's approach is to introduce students to analytical thinking. High Jump alum Alexa Ramirez noted her High Jump classes were "the first time that I was really pushed to critically think. Before then, it was all about memorization in school and that's what I did really well." Alexa remembers being told to write an argumentative essay for the first time. She could write on any topic with two opposing viewpoints. When she handed in a first draft, her teacher pointed out that all she'd submitted were facts. With time, she began to rely less on encyclopedic knowledge, and instead cultivated her unique point of view. "That's where you grow as a person," she readily admits. Benjamin Serrano, another alum, agrees. In contrast to other organizations, which solely focus on getting students' grades up, High Jump offers "more critical thinking classes that you wouldn't necessarily have in your home school."

To support this transition to analytical thinking, High Jump intentionally maintains intimate classrooms. Jess Mora, another High Jump alum, noted, "The biggest shock to me was how small the classes at High Jump were. I want to say there were no more than sixteen students per class, and that was such a big shock because I came from a public elementary school where there were thirty, thirty-two students depending on the year in my class." These larger class sizes, Jess shared, made it "hard to establish a relationship with the teacher or feel like you had someone to go to for help, so I always remember being super independent."

At High Jump, teachers and TAs (recent alumni in nearby high schools and colleges) made sure to offer consistent support to students. Jess remembers that "teachers were constantly asking you 'How is it going?' 'Is everything going okay?'" Seeing her teachers' diligent support signaled to Jess that they "really are passionate and care that you do well and that you are happy." This is the differentiator for Jess (and explains why she's remained involved as a TA since finishing the program). "Something just feels different here," Jess shared. "Yes, I'm learning material that I didn't know before, and it's at a faster pace and the resources are greater there. But I think the biggest shock for me was the sense of community and support that I felt there that I didn't feel at school."

These are heartening words for the High Jump leadership, who are very deliberate in creating this supportive environment. According to Karen Thomas, one of High Jump's campus directors, they try to both implicitly model and explicitly state the academic norms students will benefit from. The team signals some of the ways college classrooms might operate through discussion-based class structures or the routines built into different courses. By introducing this at such a young age, High Jump helps acclimate students to particular styles of class participation and how to engage with teachers and peers alike.

OFFICE HOURS: INTIMIDATION OR CULTIVATION?
The positioning and perception of teachers are some of the most powerful academic norms for which YDOs like High Jump can help students prepare. At High Jump, teachers state clearly that they exist as a resource for students. As Karen Thomas shares, during class sessions, "I'm walking around talking with the students. If you have a problem, you're coming to me; it's very much more of a community, and the kids have a say, which is how I believe school should be." This teaching approach models the idea that students benefit from cultivating relationships with teachers as resources, allies,

and supporters. College faculty certainly reward students who take this approach, but rarely make that explicit because it's assumed to be obvious.

Perhaps no other dimension of faculty-student relationships creates more uncertainty than office hours. When students start a college course, they receive a syllabus, in which faculty detail when they hold office hours. Rarely, though, do they actually explain the purpose of office hours. Dr. Jack argues that this scares off the students who might benefit most from the one-on-one attention office hours provide. As Reality Changers alumnus Jessie Hernandez-Reyes shared, office hours seemed "intimidating because I felt like I was going to be alone with a professor in their office, and that's a lot of pressure." She assumed that office hours might function like an unofficial test, somewhere "you have to prove yourself."

Those of us who have been to office hours know that they are not intended to intimidate students. Instead, they can be used for a variety of purposes, including answering students' questions on class topics, digging in further on a particular reading or discussion, or gaining advice on how to study the topic further and potentially pursue a career in the field. Jack argues that this range of possibilities is part of what muddies the water around office hours. To solve this, he argues that all faculty should define the purpose of their office hours in their syllabus and clearly reiterate that when reviewing the syllabus during the first class session.

Even then, some first-generation students note that many faculty still expect students to know how to go about asking for help when they finally do attend office hours. As one student

Dr. Rachel Gable interviews in her book *The Hidden Curriculum* shares, you need to know how to formulate an "office hour question." She interpreted the student's frustration as feeling like "he was expected to know the linguistic codes of a ritual performance when it came to the practice of office hours, and that his classmates were already well-versed in the ritual, its expectations and cadences, whereas [he] had no idea how to even begin to try." (pg 83) This student is picking up on just how deeply ingrained the hidden curriculum is, even when faculty make an effort to peel back the first layer of mystery.

ASKING FOR HELP

Part of the reason clarifying office hours is so important is that they are one of a number of essential resources that can make or break a student's academic success in college. College administrators know the academic transition to university can be challenging and thus try to make different resources available to students, including academic centers, tutoring, discussion sessions with teaching assistants, and office hours. What often gets in the way is a student's hesitation to ask for help.

This is something that Jordan Harrison at Reality Changers confronts regularly. He shares that the first three months of college are crucial for first-generation students. Students "are just blown away not only by the amount of freedom [they have], but also the amount of isolation." They struggle to navigate campus and find the right resources for which they might need support. When his students face these barriers though, they often don't inform Reality Changers staff until it's too late. Harrison believes that is because his students, especially young men of color, are "conditioned to *not* ask for help."

For students who enter some of the most elite universities, their past academic success creates an expectation for themselves that can be hard to adjust to. "Having been the tutors in their high schools, they arrived in college with the false but firm belief that one could not be both smart and need a tutor in college," Gable writes. (pg 89) She found that in contrast to first-generation students who saw academic support as a weakness, multigenerational college students proactively sought out tutors as a preventative measure. The hesitation to ask for help proves to be another immense academic barrier within the hidden curriculum.

TAKEAWAYS

These challenging dynamics speak to the broader concerns Harrison sees his students face. When they reach campus, they might be intimidated, convinced that their own experience can't match that of their peers. "Sometimes students realize what it means to come from a Title I school and go to a university where other students had these phenomenal high school experiences or had their AP classes and IB classes," he shares. "So a lot of our students sometimes go in and they say, 'I can't even compete with these students.'" In other words, here is where the imposter syndrome, discussed in Chapter 1, rears its ugly head.

Ultimately, YDOs have an opportunity to prepare students to thrive academically, by understanding how to operate successfully in the classroom and tap into available resources. In doing so, the hope is that students learn more deeply, setting themselves up for the greatest potential impact after graduation. For YDO alumni like Jess, the inputs from her YDO teachers and mentors translated into deeper engagement in her learning. At her home school, she felt disengaged, going through the motions of assignments so she got good grades, but not so she could learn. High Jump, on the other hand, challenged her. "It felt a lot more like an environment conducive to actual learning and not just getting things done for the sake of getting things done." YDOs make sure we don't take actual learning for granted, and for that, we should be grateful.

CHAPTER 6:

Social Codes of College

Jennine Capo Crucet and her whole family piled into their car to drive from her family's home in Miami to her new home at Cornell University. She writes in the *New York Times*, "Shortly after arriving on campus, the five of us—my parents, my younger sister, my abuela and me—found ourselves listening to a dean end his welcome speech with the words: 'Now, parents, please: Go!' Almost everyone in the audience laughed, but not me, and not my parents. They turned to me and said, 'What does he mean, *Go*?'"

A first-generation college family, Jennine's family thought they needed to stay through all of orientation, to support their daughter. So, for the next week, the whole family went through the motions of orientation. As the family proceeded through the week, they confronted an unexpected checklist of dorm items. "Every afternoon during that week, we had to go back to the only department store we could find, the now-defunct Ames, for some stupid thing we hadn't known was a necessity, something not in our budget: shower shoes, extra-long twin sheets, mesh laundry bags," Capo Crucet writes. "Before the other families left, we carefully watched them—they knew what they were doing—and we made new shopping lists with our limited vocabulary: *Those things that lift up the bed*, we wrote. *That plastic thing to carry stuff to the bathroom.*"

Capo Crucet's family eventually left, a week later, but her disorientation remained. "While my college had done an excellent job recruiting me, I had no road map for what I was supposed to do once I made it to campus," she writes. Capo Crucet's experience starting college illuminates the powerful social codes of college.

Understanding these college codes is like an additional item on the move-in list. Some students move into their dorms with the social codes packed along with the bed risers and extra-long sheets. Others, especially first-generation students, come to realize that, like laundry bags and shower shoes, an understanding of these codes is something to figure out. Three powerful ways that social codes manifest at college are in belongings, bureaucracy, and belonging. As with academic norms, YDOs also invest in preparing students for these dynamics, though it proves a trickier terrain to navigate.

BELONGINGS

Physical belongings can be a tangible way to signal one's wealth and the corresponding cultural capital that is deemed valuable on college campuses. From North Face and Canada Goose jackets to luxurious meals, the physical manifestations of privilege prove powerful. While these physical belongings can be a signal of one's wealth, they also prove to be self-reinforcing. They are deemed worth having and so others work to also acquire and show off those status symbols, reflecting their belonging in the in-group. Belongings can be a means to belonging.

Dr. Rachel Gable interviewed dozens of first-generation students at Harvard and Georgetown as part of her research on the hidden curriculum. Across these conversations, she heard students confess shock and anxiety around the way wealthy peers spent money and a lack of appreciation for that spending. She writes that students "described the routines of mental calculations behind poker faces: a single night out with friends compared to their entire family's monthly grocery bill; a peer's suggestion to load a metro card with fifty dollars when a single ride cost two dollars; a roommate leaving for class and returning with new boots and a four-hundred- dollar receipt." (pg 135) She notes that the wealthy neighborhoods both Georgetown and Harvard are situated within didn't help, as affordable outlets were rarely available.

One Georgetown student that Gable interviewed, Skylar, really struck a chord with me. She described arriving at Georgetown and learning about brands like J.Crew and Vineyard Vines for the first time, labels that epitomize preppy collegiate style. Boat shoes, sundresses, pastels, and floral prints abound. "Georgetown is telling you that you are amazing, and you are Georgetown, so you want to look that part." Skylar soon spent way above her means to get some of these name brands to signal her fit. One Christmas, Skylar's mom went without gifts so that she could max out the J.Crew clearance racks for her daughter. In that moment, Skylar said she felt awful for going to such extremes to try and match the habits of her wealthy peers. (pg 137)

Wealth shows up on college campuses through these many examples and more. Gaining some comfort in wealthier spaces can help ease the transition to elite schools. This is a fundamental component of the academic placement YDO model. These organizations believe that placing students into the most elite middle and high schools will offer them a familiarity with physical displays of wealth at a younger age. While there's a ready critique of these approaches advancing an unfair system (more on that in Part 3), this relative comfort in wealthy spaces does make this element of the college transition less startling. This is a fundamental component of Dr. Jack's thesis around the experience of the Privileged Poor, who benefit from gaining the cultural touchpoints of elite high schools.

Other YDO approaches try to expose students to new cultural touchpoints that might be assumed common on elite college campuses. Reality Changers does this by having their students work at cultural events in the city. Although they're occupying a working role, rather than as a participant, they are still gaining exposure to different cultural touchpoints and observing certain etiquette. In getting this experience, students gain a familiarity that can help them feel more comfortable in college, which can then positively reinforce their engagement both academically and socially.

The Let's Get Ready team partners with an organization called Grad Bag to make sure students arrive on campus with some of the physical items that foster belonging. Grad Bag helps recycle used college gear left behind when students move out of their dorms and makes them available to incoming, lower-income students. Monica Duque, a Let's

Get Ready alum and staff member, vividly remembers seeing students trying to balance bags full of their newly acquired supplies on the New York City subways. She shared that she had to encourage students who hesitated to take too much, because the reality is that students are going to "need this, but sometimes your parents really can't afford to pay for it."

BUREAUCRACY

Students who understand the social codes of elite universities not only physically pack the belongings to show that status; they're also more likely to understand how to navigate the bureaucracy of these complicated institutions. Part of the burden of academic bureaucracy is the inaccessible language used to describe academic resources. Fortunately, some vocal members of academia want to simplify the language of college administration. "There is a sense that if you're in an academic environment, writing has to be complex so that it reflects the intellectual level of a university," says Deborah Bosley, a former University of North Carolina Charlotte professor. (Johnston, 2019) She believes this is absolutely the opposite of what schools should be doing. Instead, they should view students as their primary audience and adjust the language accordingly.

Sometimes, it's as simple as eliminating wonky words and writing them more simply, even if a few more words are needed. At Texas A&M University, for example, one advocate changed the word "domicile" in a financial aid policy to instead read "to live in." Failing to correct the burdensome language on college websites threatens student opportunities. As Bosley argues, unapproachable language "is going to diminish the likelihood that [students] will be able to appropriately enroll in the university." (Johnston, 2019)

I have already discussed one great example of confusing terminology: office hours. Without clear definition, the term is foreign to anyone not steeped in the lingo of higher education. Another bureaucratic example of unusual university language is the *bursar*. The bursar is a position specific to universities that is responsible for financial affairs. They work closely with financial aid offices to ensure that students are charged and pay what is expected based on their financial aid packages. When students face billing issues, they are expected to solve it through the bursar's office. But so many first-generation students might never learn what a bursar is in the first place. YDOs and progressive high schools alike will often use the bursar's office as an example of a student resource that could provide valuable information but one that students might never know to approach. By preparing students with a run-down of different campus resources and how students might interact with them, YDOs are able to circumvent likely challenges.

For the Let's Get Ready leadership, it's not enough to only learn what a certain resource is. Having the skills to navigate nuanced conversations and challenges with university administrators is an important skill, and one that can help students avoid any barriers on the path to graduation. As Let's Get Ready CEO Lena Eberhart states, "Sure, you need to know what the bursar is. But do you know what to ask the bursar? Do you know what information they need to give you? How to be persistent when they won't answer your phone call or they don't understand your question?"

In practice, Eberhart's team has seen that though a student might know to follow up with a bursar, they may then be pushed around or left in the dark when faced with new questions or unfamiliar steps in the process.

Let's Get Ready sees their role as "catching students before something becomes a true barrier." To do that, they rely, in part, on their peer mentors to ask their mentees if essential components are taken care of well in advance of any deadlines, like ensuring bills are paid a few months early. This helps avoid unnecessary dropouts or breaks from school due to administrative error. To get them ready, mentors role-play these kinds of conversations with their student mentees. These practice conversations help prepare students to ask helpful follow-up questions and hold their ground until they get necessary clarity. This serves as another example of how YDO interventions can offer overlooked but hugely important skills to students.

BELONGING

The social codes can be influential in ensuring that students have the tangible possessions and skills they need to navigate the practicalities of college life. But the power of social codes is most influential in how it informs students' sense of belonging. It's important for students to find their fit on campus. When they don't, they are less likely to tap into available campus resources or opportunities. These missed opportunities can snowball, with students just going through the motions of college. The consequence, Dr. Jack explains, is that students "who delay integrating into the larger college community also have less access to social support from their peers and from the college as a whole—support that proves crucial to success both in college and in the labor market upon graduation." (pg 28) Facing norms that feel unfamiliar can be othering, undermining efforts to gel on campus.

With this shift comes a new set of rules that students pick up on. As High Jump alumna Jess shared, "The school environment is now very different and there's these little rules that you feel like you have to learn in order to navigate this new world." Jess went so far as to say there was a "playbook" for her school, and if you could follow the rules set out in that playbook, you'd probably be able to coast along. But the process of learning these norms and deciding how you want to approach them is a complex and emotionally draining expectation placed on students.

Many YDOs recognize how taxing this can be and work to prepare students to handle these social dynamics just as they do for academic demands. All of the organizations I spoke with emphasized social connection and building community, particularly with peers of a shared experience or identity. Relationships with peers who carry similar values and priorities can prove a powerful counterweight to taxing social dynamics. YDOs do this in part by modeling what community can look and feel like. As an organization that's closely woven into the community in San Diego, Reality Changers offers a family-like feel for its students. Beyond the routine of the after-school sessions, the program also offers a free meal to students. Students literally come together for a meal as family.

Another powerful element of YDO communities is the reflection of adults with similar backgrounds as students. Many alumni I spoke with noted that they had an extra level of comfort at their YDO because they knew that the teachers or tutors they worked with understood intimately some of the same challenges they faced. Unlike many of her peers, Jessie Reyes-Hernandez joined the Reality Changers community later in high school and worried she'd feel out of place. Fortunately, her connection with teachers helped her. She shared, "I felt that I was supported because the instructors were also from a first gen background, and they had my best intentions in mind." As a result, Jessie felt comfortable then connecting with the rest of the community and buying into the organization's offerings.

If instructors can be positive influences from a distance, then tutors and mentors closer in age can be particularly formative. Let's Get Ready's near-peer model very intentionally focuses on social belonging. Much of Let's Get Ready's approach utilizes nudges—small, targeted and intentionally timed reminders to help students stay on track with academic and personal developmental goals. The leadership readily acknowledges though, that while they see great value in the nudges, the pairing of students with near-peer mentors is an impactful complement. Managing Director of Program Design Grace Bianciardi explains that all peer mentors are trained to prioritize discussions on social belonging and to specifically assess and track their mentee's progress in building social connections.

While the team at Let's Get Ready touts the value of social connection, they also insist it doesn't just happen passively. Finding meaningful social connection requires intentionality and proactive outreach. As part of their college prep sessions, facilitators discuss how to anticipate culture shock. Community building is reinforcing that "breaking down the myth that you're just going to show up on campus and your people are going to be there, that it's going to be like the catalogue."

Instead, Let's Get Ready leaders and peer mentors emphasize that loneliness is a common experience in the college transition process and that building relationships requires intentional effort. To get ahead of this, facilitators prompt Let's Get Ready students to consider the kinds of friends they've had in the past, how they met them and why they found those relationships meaningful. Students are encouraged to reflect on their values and then proactively seek out student clubs and campus events that are most likely to attract people that align with students' hopes. These sessions ensure students can build relationships, which build their resilience and offer support in navigating college, whether academic or social dynamics.

WHOSE COMMUNITY IS IT ANYWAY?

Once students do recognize the power of social codes on campus, they quickly confront what those codes are grounded in: the white, wealthy experience. In unpacking the experiences of the Privileged Poor, Jack explains that wealthier and multi-generational students have an advantage because "the norms they learned at home are the same ones that govern campus life—norms such as looking someone in the eye while giving a firm handshake, feeling entitled to adults' time and being proactive in forging relationships with authority figures." (pg 19) For students from less-resourced high schools, the opportunities available on campus may be entirely unfamiliar and intimidating, dressed in the trappings of wealth they've never experienced first-hand.

For many students of color, attending a predominantly white institution can be the first time they're made to feel in the minority. As Gable describes in her book *The Hidden Curriculum*, many first-generation students of color at Harvard and Georgetown came from majority minority schools and communities. One student, Reyna, grew up in a segregated neighborhood and school, so she never felt in the minority growing up. But once she arrived at college, she came to feel she "was in a racial and socioeconomic bubble that I didn't realize would cause such a crisis when I got here." She suddenly had to confront the jarring, othering experience of being the only Black student in some of her classes and social groups. (Gable, pg 130)

Students pick up on the dominance of white, wealthy norms. One of the students Jack features in *The Privileged Poor* acknowledged that she code-switched in college in order to "gain citizenship in a rich, white place." (pg18) One way colleges and YDOs respond is to prepare students about these norms and equip them with the tools to reflect their understanding of them, if not ascribe to them. The risk here is that in an effort to foster greater social connectivity, these efforts might perpetuate a narrow, exclusive understanding of what college culture is and can be.

Alumni of YDO programs readily acknowledge that adapting to these new norms is challenging and an area YDOs can continue to improve on. High Jump alum Jess noted that while she found great community within the program, there was some risk that that sense of community could also be misleading. She worried that High Jump students who largely end up going to predominantly white, private, and parochial schools might believe their future classrooms would feel just like a High Jump classroom. But as she attests, when they enter high school, "the shift is very obvious. These are predominantly white schools where you don't have a lot of people who look like you physically or socio-economically."

TAKEAWAYS

These challenging dynamics are a fundamental element of the hidden curriculum. While the skill building, role-playing, and anticipation of upcoming challenges are all valuable lessons YDOs offer, students will still confront the realities of how their identities show up in college spaces. We can't assume that if students are taught about these norms and choose to adopt them (a tough decision on its own), that suddenly the difficulties of the college transition will disappear.

Dr. Marcia Chatelain, the Georgetown professor who launched the Hidden Curriculum course mentioned in Chapter 1, makes sure her peers, and particularly university leadership, understand this. She recognizes the risk in how people view her course. Dr. Chatelain very intentionally signals that her course is not "an intensive etiquette lesson, designed to tell students to adopt the practices of an elite class in order to mask their disadvantage or confusion."

She is clear with her colleagues and university administrators that her course is a temporary bridge, but not a long-term solution. "We cannot address inequality with a crash course on manners; we need more tutorials on power. First-generation advocates have to listen to our students' critiques, take their protests seriously, and understand their perspective on what is lost when opportunities are gained," Chatelain asserts. "The reality is that no matter how well-intentioned such initiatives are, they are not a salve for the sting of racism and classism that has yet to be fully acknowledged, let alone confronted, in the academy."

Like many YDO leaders, Chatelain understands her role as providing a model and showing students "that another higher education is possible, one in which a parent's alumni status or connections or wealth are not the only ways to realize success." As students increasingly gain the language and confidence to insist they have support around race and identity in their education, YDOs are realizing they need to invest more in this work.

CHAPTER 7:

The Power of Self-Efficacy

―

My freshman year, I'm squeezing my best friend's hand, palm sweating, as we anxiously await the results of the Model UN conference, our first since joining the college team. My sophomore year, I'm working side by side with my psychology professor, parsing through data from a recent experiment that we're hoping will become the professor's next great paper. My junior year, I'm grimacing at the bitter taste of a Tuborg beer on my very first night studying abroad in Copenhagen, Denmark, living in a commune with eighty Danish students. My senior year, I'm nervously laughing at a group of middle schoolers awaiting my lesson in sexual health, the culmination of my internship with Planned Parenthood's education team.

Four years, four very different stories. But there's one connective thread: self-efficacy. I was able to unlock each of these by proactively finding opportunities and taking chances to engage in them. This proactive approach is also known as self-efficacy, a belief in one's independent abilities. Self-efficacy is the common denominator across YDOs. No matter the approach they take or the students they serve, every YDO I spoke with emphasized their commitment to building the sense of resilience and proactiveness in their students. Why is this such an important trait to foster?

Advocating for yourself is a powerful action both in academic and social settings. Whether seeking out counsel in office hours or support from counselors for mental health care, a proactive approach to one's experience at college can be powerful. It can make the difference between just getting through college and squeezing every possible opportunity to learn and grow out of college. It's what the most privileged students do to make the most of their university experience, and YDOs know other students can do that too.

In other words, it is a powerful element of the hidden curriculum, with privileged students benefiting from that knowledge and trait. YDOs know this, which is exactly why they're motivated to level the playing field for their own students with less privilege and great promise. I'm focusing on this particular trait in this chapter because it also connects and reinforces so many other elements of the hidden curriculum I've discussed, from admissions and academic norms to social codes.

EMBRACE ENTITLEMENT

The need to build self-efficacy in students is the most consistent priority across the YDOs I featured. In some cases, the YDOs demonstrate a bias, whether stated or implied, in selecting students who demonstrate the ability to advocate for themselves. In many other cases, building skills around speaking up and being your own booster is prioritized in the program model.

The latter is true for Let's Get Ready. "We know for some people there is a stronger sense of belonging than others right off the bat," CEO Lena Eberhart explains. "But it is normal to encounter [in college] a lot of things you don't quite understand or you don't have experience with. So we think about how can you normalize that so you emotionally feel prepared to move through it." Part of how they normalize this is by using peer mentors. By deploying peer mentors as partners, Let's Get Ready focuses on building students' comfort and confidence in proactively seeking out what they need on campus.

Eberhart is clear when approaching self-efficacy work. This is about building a sense of entitlement that's usually missing from strivers.[4] She wants students to think "I'm entitled to the information I need to be successful. It is within my power to get that information. And there are ways to seek it that are more successful than others." Those are the skills Let's Get Ready is hyper-focused on building in students.

If you're like me, you might recoil at the idea of building a sense of entitlement in students. In common speech, it carries a deeply negative connotation. I envision a bratty, petulant child, a haughty, nose-in-the-air snob, when I think of someone who is entitled. However, educators like Eberhart intentionally use the term to try and call out the fact

---

4 "Strivers" is a term Dr. Jennifer Morton uses in her book *Moving Up Without Losing Your Way* to describe first-generation, low-income, and non-traditional students who are striving for success.

that wealthier, more privileged peers are approaching their education in an entitled way.

I felt that viscerally when I moved to my high school in Newton, Massachusetts. Students knew they were due a great education and insisted on it from the school; often that fell down the slippery slope of demanding higher grades and padded resumes to help with college applications, even if their performance wasn't up to snuff. But the fact remains that my peers knew, thanks to conditioning from their community, that to get ahead they had to speak up for themselves. The reputation of Newton is so strong that Susan Johnson, the Boston area high school counselor, tells her students to be like "that Newton kid." She encourages her students to "act like everything belongs to you, act like everything is yours, because everyone around you will."

The Newton kid is a powerful example for teachers like Johnson to use, because they generally adhere to the archetype colleges were built around. The archetypal student is one who easily knows what they want and need, advocates for it and capitalizes on any resources available to them. These archetypal students brim with confidence; they are their own best advocate. But the archetype in mind is also a white, wealthy male. This might not be surprising given just how recently many colleges were exclusively white or male.[5] YDOs understand that history and

---

5   Take Wesleyan University, a prestigious liberal arts college, as an example. Though the college was founded in 1831, it did not begin accepting women into its four-year undergraduate degree programs until 1970. (Tomkiw) When the Supreme Court's decision in Brown v. Board of Education desegregated all schools by law in 1957, Harvard College only had one Black student in its graduating class. These legacies remain relatively recent history.

know it must be chipped away at. One way they can do that is by ensuring that every student operates like those Newton kids.

SELF-EFFICACY IN PRACTICE

Though it might feel icky to say, entitlement is a powerful force at universities. Students who made it to college have paid for (or financial aid has covered) the services the college has to offer. This ranges from student services like mental health counseling or student clubs to practical resources like quality housing, library access, and research databases. The most fundamental component of a university—its teaching— is a service that students and their families have bought into. Wealthier students operate with an understanding of this, one where faculty are almost seen as service providers. As Jess observed at her private high school, students held a belief that "teachers are working for me."

If students at private high schools carry this over to college, then the system will reward them. Sure, there's a way to be obnoxiously entitled and most faculty I know won't tolerate outright brattiness. But there's a fine line between being seen as condescendingly entitled and admirably self-advocating. Faculty understand that students are owed a certain amount of support; the existence of office hours reflects that. As Let's Get Ready leader Grace Bianciardi states, professors "are hired in order to go to office hours with you and help you understand" class content. She and other YDO leaders want to make clear to students that the power of self-efficacy runs deep.

Despite this messaging, some students have a hard time wrapping their heads around that. Many first-generation, low-income students, in particular, struggle to reconcile the narratives of their youth with what they're taught to believe in college. When she was working on her own book about the experiences of first-generation students, Jess found these clashing narratives to cause real conflict. A common refrain she heard in interviews was "I'm low-income, but I'm not poor." These students would think, "Okay, I could use that resource but there's probably someone out there who needs it a lot more than I do. So I'm not going to take that laptop or ask for that extra money because there's probably another person who could use it more."

But Jess understood that this has a compounding effect on the resources available to all students of higher financial need. "The reality is that if all students do that, no one's ever going to take advantage of that resource," she shared/ "And if the resources allocated for, for example, first-gen, low-income students or students of color aren't used, it's hard to advocate from a staff or faculty perspective for more money." She clearly understood, from her own journey of building self-efficacy and tapping into the resources available to her, that not doing so would cost many students potentially life-changing opportunities. Her main message to fellow first-generation, low-income students is to be upfront about what you need, because "it's impossible for professors or advisors to really know what you need and how to best help you."

SELF-EFFICACY IS SELF-REINFORCING

I'm particularly struck by YDOs' consistent focus on self-efficacy because I can clearly see how a proactive approach enabled some of the most formative experiences for me and my peers. This self-efficacy not only can smooth out challenges in academic and social circles; it can unlock high-impact educational opportunities like learning communities, research, fellowship, internship opportunities, and study abroad.[6] In striving for these opportunities, students will find many of the same admissions, academic, and social dynamics of the hidden curriculum reemerge. This is exactly why learning about the hidden curriculum can be a game changer; gaining these skills and awareness can offer the maximum opportunities from college.

Student Organizations

In the research on high-impact practices, engaging with learning communities is usually framed around classes that are linked consecutively and framed around a "real world problem." (Kuh, 2021) I'll use my creative license here and identify learning communities as extending beyond that, namely through extracurricular student-led organizations. Any student who has attended the student org fairs during college orientation knows just how many options for engagement are available. Identity-based groups, interest-based groups, service organizations, fraternities and sororities, competitive groups, or intramural sports all offer opportunities to engage with peers in a structured way outside of the classroom.

To someone who has participated in a group like this before, the benefits might seem obvious. But that's not always clear to new students, especially when academics and college prep

---

6   Dr. George D. Kuh details a number of "high impact educational opportunities" that inform a great deal of different educational interventions.

activities consumed their attention. As YDO alum Jessie Reyes-Hernandez shares, "As first-gen students, you're trying so hard to get through college, that no one really tells you that you should also be involved in extracurricular activities." Yet they can offer a healthy balance to academic life, help cultivate professional skills, and sow new networks. In Dr. Gable's research of students at Harvard and Georgetown, students with strong commitments to one or two extracurriculars consistently felt more satisfied socially than those who did not.

These benefits are sometimes masked by gatekeeping to participate in certain groups. While many student organizations welcome anyone, some require an application process that can feel jarring after finally getting past the college admissions process. Gaining entry into exclusive clubs can require a rehashing of the same dynamics as the admissions process. This is particularly true at the most elite institutions. In *The Hidden Curriculum*, Gable shares the story of a student frustrated by having to compete for a spot in the extracurriculars he was most interested in. "He spoke of the sting associated with working so hard in high school to achieve the reward of admission to an elite college, only to discover that admission did not confer access to the social life promised in glossy brochures." Gable writes, "He would have to apply, compete, and prove himself all over again." (pg 109) Students spoke with Gable about concerns that the selections processes for exclusive organizations were perpetuating the unfair structures that they were trying to overcome academically.

When students can find community in student organizations, though, it can be deeply impactful. Gable particularly finds this in ethnic-identity student groups. For first generation students of color, she writes, "Ethnic organizations were important sources of social connection and comfort in the often unfamiliar terrain of a college campus." (pg 107) One unstated benefit of these groups is that younger students can learn from older students in the organizations. They become peer mentors, trusted to offer frank advice and insights based on their own experiences navigating this worn terrain. Like the structured near-peer model from Let's Get Ready, this informal mentoring can help students anticipate roadblocks and more smoothly steer around them.

Study Abroad

Many students might come into college knowing that an option to study abroad exists. They just don't necessarily believe it's an option for them. Whether it's the financial burden, the idea of being far from family who might rely on them, or fear the experience would derail their timely graduation, many students end up never even considering study abroad. Students who can proactively build relationships though, might get guidance from mentors to show what options are available to them after all.

Study abroad struggles to engage the full diversity of college students. According to Diversity Abroad, students of color represent 46 percent of students enrolled in colleges and universities but only 29 percent of students who pursue education abroad. (2019) In Dr. Gable's research, she consistently found that first-generation students who did study abroad consistently noted it was transformative.

For some of the students Gable interviewed, the ability to get away from campus helped them reset how they approached the campus culture. One student shared, "I feel like [on campus] there has been a culture established where you have to be involved in X, Y, and Z. I know the first two years I felt that pressure. Not so much anymore. Going abroad changed that for me. When I got back, I chose to participate in activities that I found truly fulfilling." Another student felt she could shake "this whole 'I don't belong here' feeling" when she spent a semester abroad. (Gable, pg 69)

In both these examples, study abroad acts as the release on the pressure valve. Though everything abroad is new and perhaps overwhelming, that's true for everyone. First-generation and other underrepresented students aren't alone in that experience. In fact, the resilience and adaptability that they used in adjusting to college can be a great asset while studying abroad.

Study abroad offers a positive reframe for a lot of the coping skills marginalized students develop in navigating college environments. Code-switching provides an excellent example of this. Wagaye Johannes, a leader at Diversity Abroad, shared that for students who already code-switch, "if you're going to a new country you actually have the skill set to figure out how to maneuver a new country versus someone that has been in the same sort of cultural bubble." This is a great example of how Johannes and her colleagues take a strength-based approach to reframe often marginalized experiences as real assets while studying abroad.

For students to unlock study abroad opportunities, they need to be proactive in researching available study abroad options, sort out financial aid, and pursue an application. When they do, they reap the benefits. According to Gable, study abroad "led to a deepened commitment toward a major or academic path, reduced stress upon return to campus…and an expansion of the sense of possibilities for their future careers and how they wished to balance their personal and professional lives." (pg 69)

Research, Fellowship, & Internship Opportunities

While student organizations can be overwhelming to join, there is at least a similar structure in most high schools. Study abroad also follows a familiar academic schedule and structure, even if the experience of living abroad can be dizzying. The precedent does not exist in the same way for more professionally oriented opportunities. Research assistantships, fellowships, and internships are three common opportunities college students can unlock, but they can feel like a black box for unfamiliar students. Self-advocacy can go a long way in helping to decipher these hidden codes.

For starters, what even are these opportunities? At most universities, faculty are expected to do research in their fields in addition to teaching. Research assistant positions offer students the opportunity to work alongside faculty to support their latest research. While science labs might come to mind when hearing this, there are research opportunities in every field.

Fellowships are an even broader category. These are usually funded opportunities to focus on a particular experience or passion project; fellowships can take place during college or after graduation. Examples include teaching English abroad as a Fulbright Scholar, pursuing graduate studies in the UK as a Rhodes or Marshall Scholar, or conducting research as a Sloan Foundation Research Fellow. Though these may sound similar to a scholarship, fellows receive money in order to undertake some kind of project or work. Many fellowships offer a helpful pathway into new careers and professional networks.

Internships are the most familiar of these opportunities. Interns work within professional organizations to support the business and learn about the industry and organization they're supporting. These can be paid or unpaid and range in time commitments from five hours a week to a full-time forty hour per week job; in the summers during college years, many students pursue internships as a means of boosting their post-graduate career prospects.

Broadly, these kinds of opportunities tend to go to more privileged students. According to a National Association of Colleges and Employers study that examined how many students of different races held paid internships, white students were overrepresented in paid internships, while Black students were underrepresented. Hispanic-American students were unfortunately overrepresented in the category of having no internships. These statistics signal a broader, but unsurprising, reality that in America, students of color face additional barriers in accessing important professional opportunities like internships.

Though these three types of opportunities are quite different, each requires a generally similar approach. Peter Raucci advises students at The Posse Foundation, a national academic placement YDO, on graduate school and fellowship opportunities. He laid out a helpful framework in approaching these kinds of opportunities: 1) know what opportunities and programs exist; 2) understand admissions requirements and gain confidence of getting in; and 3) find the right alignment between your experience and goals and the available programs.

Self-efficacy proves a crucial skill at each of these three stages. As Raucci suggested in step one, those students who are proactive in seeking out information are more likely to learn about these kinds of opportunities. Research assistantships can come from building a relationship with a professor or speaking up in class. I wasn't especially good at going to office hours and focusing on relationship building, but a professor of mine pulled me aside halfway through the semester to ask if I'd be interested in pursuing research, largely because I actively participated in a normally passive lecture course.

Finding internship and fellowship opportunities often come about through contacts with peers and alumni of your school. Students who are proactive in meeting with counselors in the career center or leadership office, attending campus events, or connecting with student organizations are all more likely to tap into internship opportunities available through the college's network. In these examples, we see that a sense of self-efficacy helps students engage with initial resources— like faculty at office hours or career counselors. This self-efficacy is then positively reinforced by these experiences, and new relationships help open up new opportunities like internships or research roles.

Unfortunately, the students who could most benefit from meeting with career counselors do not always feel comfortable in these settings. That was the case for Jessie Reyes-Hernandez, who was disappointed by what she described as an "impersonal" reception from her university's career center. The person reviewing her resume handed her a standard booklet and directed her to adapt her resume to fit those styles. As a first-generation student, she was hoping for more intensive, hands-on support and guidance.

In this moment, Jessie was fortunate to have a supportive YDO network to turn to. She turned to mentors back at Reality Changers to support her professional development and participated in workshops for alumni on skills like shaping your LinkedIn profile and networking. "I would go because I knew that it was a safe space for me, and it was home for me essentially," Jessie shared. She knew that she "would get support that I needed" at Reality Changers in a way that she didn't trust from her university.

The guidance of experienced mentors and professional resources are important in navigating the application requirements of these opportunities. In addition, the relationships built in the process of gaining access to these opportunities will also be essential in applying for them. Many internships and fellowships require letters of recommendation from faculty or staff who can speak to a student's work, commitment and achievements. This can prove to be a tough barrier for students who haven't cultivated relationships with potential recommenders.

The sage advice of advisors, older peers, and professors can also prove essential in finding alignment with the right opportunities. I know when I was in college, I tended to want to apply to everything. I saw a cool opportunity (and often corresponding prestige) and that signaled to me that it was worth applying for. I was frequently rejected though, because I had not done my homework to find those opportunities which were actually aligned to my interests and goals. Raucci urges his students to strive for this alignment and invest in those opportunities rather than casting a wide net with no strategy behind it.

TAKEAWAYS
All the examples above capture how an approach of self-efficacy can unlock numerous opportunities in college. Participating in student organizations, studying abroad, or securing an internship or fellowship all prove to be high impact experiences that can lead to deeper learning and lasting skills. This, in turn, makes a student more competitive for professional opportunities after graduating. There is a snowball effect, as with each great opportunity unlocked, more prospects emerge.

Self-efficacy proves powerful in securing these at a macro-level, but also unlocks them starting at smaller levels. A proactive approach to office hours or building social connections can also snowball, building one's confidence to then more doggedly pursue other, larger opportunities.

While I've framed this possibility very positively here, the inverse is true. For students who aren't aware of how much self-efficacy is rewarded at American colleges, they will struggle to gain in the ways more proactive peers will. This is exactly why YDOs do and should continue to invest so heavily in building this trait in their students. In a system that rewards the go-getter, an investment in greater self-efficacy can help students gain access to those opportunities that level the playing field. But the playing field remains rigged, no matter how many YDO lessons there are.

PART 3

In the preceding chapters, we've seen evidence that the American educational system is broken, and a powerful hidden curriculum of unstated norms, behaviors, and language make the system even harder to negotiate. Youth development organizations help students deal with the system by teaching and translating the hidden curriculum. These YDOs are positioned to introduce, analyze, and translate these unspoken norms and institutional cultures for their students. It's an important responsibility that's often overlooked, assumed to be a shared mandate between public schools and parents. Though they cannot possibly meet the needs of all students left behind by the formal education system, YDOs deserve recognition for the thousands of students they do help.

In the face of these overwhelming barriers, YDOs are confronted with some challenging questions: Who should we serve? How can we best serve them? Should we try to maximize our reach or deepen our impact on a select few? The answers to these questions start to shape how each YDO approaches their work and reveals how YDOs believe they can tackle the larger educational inequities our country faces.

In all my interviews across almost a dozen YDOs, though, one question proved most challenging: *Do I best prepare my students for their education and future by helping them navigate this broken system or by transforming the system for them and others?*

The answer most YDO leaders arrive at is "We need both approaches." YDOs choose to equip individual students with the tools, knowledge and awareness of how to make it through a system unfriendly to them. And YDOs also work together with students to reform the systems that routinely work against them. While some organizations are firmly anchored in one approach, most land in the messy middle. They try to both prepare students to navigate these systems and gradually change them along the way.

In these final six chapters, I'll explore how the staff, students, and alumni that make up YDOs manage these dynamics. I'll detail at the broadest levels what some of the realities are for students and the resulting decisions and outcomes for YDOs. I'll specifically consider how these decision points inform program design and pedagogy, the narratives YDOs use, and the way language is utilized in programs. Finally, I'll reflect on how the industry might have an opportunity to collectively respond in a more coordinated way. In this section, you'll hear more of my voice and analysis as I address the many questions and choices YDOs grapple with and make sense of the many conversations around tackling inequity more directly.

CHAPTER 8:

From Navigation to Transformation

In her book, *Moving Up Without Losing Your Way*, Dr. Jennifer Morton writes, "Optimists think that education has the power to transform lives; pessimists point out that this is the exception rather than the rule." (pg 2) The YDO leaders I spoke with complicate this, because I see both the optimism and pessimism in them. I sensed many of them felt both worn down by the constant injustices their students and communities face and yet buoyed by those students who have reached their goals thanks in part to the YDO's support.

The relative balance of my own pessimism and optimism about educational opportunities directly informs my perspective on how to strike a balance between a navigational and transformational approach to youth development work. On the one hand, I see, pessimistically, how the system works against so many underrepresented students; gaining the skills to navigate it will help students triumph despite the system working against them. Yet my optimism drives my belief that education can really make the difference in a young person's life. This makes me want to see the system overhauled to work for every student, not just the privileged. These same feelings manifest in the work of YDOs.

DEFINING THE NAVIGATIONAL APPROACH

"You gotta play the game." "Those are the rules of the game." "That's just how the game goes." After hearing variations of this metaphor of "the game" endlessly across interviews, I couldn't ignore it. Alumni and administrators alike picked up on the idea that there are prevailing rules that they believe need to be learned to make it through one's education and career. A navigational approach encourages students to understand the hidden curriculum and then learn how to adapt and fit in.

Let's apply this to the example of the hidden curriculum around office hours. YDOs can teach their students that office hours are a resource available to students and that they are expected to proactively attend office hours and cultivate a relationship with professors. Even if the professor doesn't explain this to them or the syllabus only makes vague allusions to the purpose, students should focus on using their knowledge to build that rapport with faculty. In the long run, that relationship building benefits students academically and professionally. By sharing this insider knowledge, the YDOs help students navigate college academics and relationships by making the hidden curriculum less of a mystery.

If a YDO took a strictly navigational approach, they would say that the priority for students is to understand these "rules of the game" and adapt to them. A more transformational approach would suggest that it's the concept of office hours that need to change and become more accessible. For example, those YDOs might suggest that faculty are responsible for clarifying the purpose of office hours and proactively making themselves available. Students could be equipped with the skills to lobby for these changes and serve as a leader amongst their peers.

NARROW PATHS TO NAVIGATE
The navigational approach is appealing in part because it is tangible and actionable. YDOs can illuminate common barriers within and outside the classroom, and then equip students with the skills to effectively overcome those barriers. This means more students can progress in their education than otherwise would without a YDO's intervention. The downside of this is that educators are outlining a narrow path on which students can succeed. This path is the one that skirts around or overcomes the obstacles they face. In other words, they're given the tools to walk part of the path of the most privileged.

In defining a narrow path, YDO educators might risk creating a sense that one's identity needs to fit a specific definition in order to stay on this path. Dr. Morton shares the story of Jeron, a college administrator who had a remarkable journey to college and his current career. Jeron grew up in Texas in a low-income community; his mother struggled with a drug addiction, and they lived on very little. He got a lucky break when his high school football coach helped him secure a college scholarship that set him on the path to his current role supporting first-generation students at an elite college. This role has helped him reflect on his own path and what it required of him.

Morton explains that in Jeron's case, "Learning to adapt to college didn't mean just figuring out how to use a bigger library, take notes more effectively, or prioritize paper writing over partying. For Jeron, adaptation required learning how to present himself differently. He had to learn to change his very demeanor, the basic way that he related to other people. He discovered that there was a vast gap between the norms he had grown up with and those he encountered in college." (Morton, pg 63)

At the broadest level, when students learn about the hidden curriculum, they realize that there's an "ideal" way of operating. That ideal is grounded in the framework of the wealthier, whiter institutions, rather than those of "disadvantaged communities." Jeron confronted this head-on and recognized that he changed in response to that ideal he felt. Other stakeholders at the university, including faculty, teaching assistants, and other students, will likely positively reinforce those changes if it means a student presents more familiarly to them. YDOs strike a difficult balance, between equipping students with navigational skills without diminishing or disregarding their fundamental identity.

This dominant ideal also creates a pressure of perfectionism. When students are accepted into an academic placement organization, for example, they come to understand that they're now representatives not only of themselves or their families, but of the YDO's brand. This can add pressure on students, and they may feel the need to change the way they present themselves. This might all compound if the student is also one of very few people on campus with their identity; students might feel like they're also representing their race or religion on top of these other pressures.

That was certainly the case for Yasmine Jaffier-Williams, an alumnus of A Better Chance (ABC). Raised in Brooklyn in a Caribbean family, Yasmine was placed at a community school in Wellesley, Massachusetts, a wealthy suburb much like the one my high school was in. The program placed Yasmine with a handful of other ABC students, all of whom lived in a shared home with a teacher and her family supervising them. Yasmine felt "this sense of being perfect and making sure that you are putting your best foot forward...wherever you go, because you know you're representing a program, and anything you do is reflective of the program. We all understood that the minute we got in there."

I couldn't help hear Yasmine say this and read between the lines that being perfect meant being less of herself. She confirmed my suspicions when talking about how much she needed to adjust to the culture of the program, and in particular, the politics of her house. "I didn't understand how my specific house worked, and how to play politics in that way," Yasmine explained. "I didn't know how to do that because I'm a pretty authentic and straightforward person. But that's not necessarily going to work with this type of program."

For Yasmine, this pressure to be perfect was reinforced by the risk of losing out on the opportunity A Better Chance had offered her. Yasmine clearly understood the stakes, saying,

"Everything you've been working for in middle school and dedicating all your middle school hours, that can be taken away from you." I couldn't help but wince at the level of pressure someone could feel about the sacrifices they made as a pre-teen. This is just another reminder of how unfair it is that a young woman of color like Yasmine had to invest hundreds more hours than her wealthy, white Wellesley peers to unlock this educational opportunity, and then endure much more pressure than her peers to keep that up.

Yasmine was aware of the unfair amount of pressure placed on her. In ABC, she knew that "there's fifty people to hold you accountable for your actions, and if you do something that is not liked, then you know you get in trouble. I don't know if it's the same with other programs, or with someone in high school as a normal student." Even as I write, I remain stuck on the phrase she uses: a normal student. Though she used it in passing, I believe it reflects a deeper orientation. If her privileged peers in Wellesley are the normal ones, then she is the abnormal one. This is exactly the kind of subliminal messaging baked into the hidden curriculum, one that implies that those who don't fit the median, white, wealthy norm have to work to better align themselves with it. An orientation like this can be very damaging, wearing away at a young person's confidence and sense of self.

With that reality in mind, I began to wonder what A Better Chance's role in all this was. Yasmine was crystal clear in saying that she wasn't trying to criticize ABC. They had given her an incredible opportunity, and despite its challenges, it prepared her for her time in college. She feels confident in her college classes, thrives with some of the independence she has today. But in preparing Yasmine to navigate a predominantly white and wealthy school system, ABC may have unknowingly perpetuated some harmful pressures. This illuminates the challenging decision points YDOs face as they determine their program approach, needing to balance skill-building without creating undue pressure on their students.

PROGRESS IS NOT INEVITABLE

Most YDO approaches land somewhere between a strict navigational and strict transformational approach. Those that tend to favor a more navigational approach don't ignore systemic change. Instead, they assume that students enter institutions and change them from within, that they reach behind them to bring their families, communities and kids like them along for their upward social climb.

This is especially true of academic placement organizations. Take the example of Prep for Prep, the New York City-based organization that places primarily students of color in private schools across the city. Their measure of success is how many Prep for Prep students are able to get into these schools, excel there, and then gain entry into some of the most elite universities. These students are trained to excel in these elite educational spaces by Prep for Prep, which shares academic and social preparation tools with students. Students are prepared to navigate these unfamiliar spaces, not change them.

YDOs assume that change comes with time. They're playing a long game. This approach hinges on the belief that once students who go through Prep for Prep and similar programs graduate from college, they'll enter prestigious (and perhaps profitable) professions with likely economic success. This will officially mark their upward social mobility. It's assumed that once there, these individuals will reflect on their journey to get there. Frustrated by all the hoops they had to jump through to make it to this point, these individuals will then work to change the systems they have influence over to become more accessible for young people from a similar background.

In theory, this sounds fantastic and impactful. But how true this is in practice is almost impossible to measure and built on shaky assumptions. YDOs are limited in the impacts they're able to measure; usually they will focus on statistics immediately related to program outcomes, like how many students graduate from high school, gain admission to college, and their GPAs in school. These are time-bound, specific, and relatively easily gathered.

The same cannot be said for measuring the longer-term claims YDOs assert. It would be very difficult to track alumni of a program like Prep for Prep twenty years into their careers. Even if you could, it would be difficult to decide how to measure that. Imagine the hypothetical survey questions twenty years later: "How many young people from a background like yours have you helped in your career? In what ways have you shaped your industry to be more inclusive?" YDOs could gain interesting stories, but the causal link from the YDO's program to an individual's influence over an industry or workplace would be loose and anecdotal.

This is not all to say that YDOs shouldn't pursue a transformational agenda—quite the opposite. My concern is that most YDOs seem to believe that the influences they have on students today will *inevitably* shift ecosystems for the better. Parents, donors, and eventually students buy into this narrative as well. But it's the presumption of inevitability that causes me concern.

Progress in our education system is not guaranteed. By passively assuming systems change will happen, rather than actively prioritizing it in the short-term, YDOs risk being complicit in the continued inequalities of our educational system. Dr. Jennifer Morton warns that striving young people, like YDO alumni, find success, but in turn "risk complicity in perpetuating the structural conditions that disadvantage other strivers like themselves and potentially entrench inequality and poverty in communities like their own." (Morton, pg 98-99) There is a risk that alumni, as they gain power, will in turn reinforce the same norms that reinforce the painful power dynamics that caused them to have to strive in the first place. In this way, the cycle of inequity continues.

Morton cites her own professional ascendance as an example of this. In her early years as a professor, she found herself reenacting the styles of teaching that most informed her as a student. That meant that she would lecture "and then would let those students who were already confident enough to raise their hands and make their voices heard monopolize the discussions. That's what was expected of me, and it was the easiest thing to do." With more teaching experience, including training on more inclusive classroom practices, Morton began to recognize how her approach was reinforcing the exact same barriers she had worked against as a first-generation Latina student. She admits that in rewarding the most assertive students, she was creating an environment that "feels unwelcoming to those strivers who feel out of place on a college campus." (pg 102) In sharing her story, Morton illuminates just how easy it can be to reinforce the structures and norms of the institutions you've navigated through, to the detriment of those who, like your former self, don't know how to decode it.

TAKEAWAYS

In acknowledging the powerful "rules of the game," YDOs' navigational approaches offer students a helpful outlet to keep up in educational institutions. When offering these navigational tools, though, YDOs sometimes constrict what the pathway to succeed might look like. This can amplify the pressures that marginalized students already feel in trying to fit into the narrow definition of an ideal student. The navigational approach also assumes a certain inevitable form of systemic change, one that believes the students who benefit from YDO programming will remain committed to systems change. In reality, as YDO alumni succeed, they may decide it's safest to not rock the boat and instead fully conform to the existing structures, which means young people of similar backgrounds will continue to struggle.

In this way, Dr. Morton's reflection on optimism and pessimism is fitting. YDO leaders who use a navigational methodology have the pessimism to know the rules of the game are powerful in an unfair way. They teach about these rules hidden between the lines because they fear students who don't learn them will be denied opportunities. Yet they have the optimism to believe that their program support will lead to lasting change. Interestingly, a very different set of optimistic and pessimistic outlooks informs the transformative approach as well.

CHAPTER 9:

...To Transformation

The deep sighs. The knowing looks. The slow head nods. The shifting of weight in their seats. The slumped shoulders. The wrinkle of noses. In each of my interviews with YDO leaders, I saw a noticeable shift in body language as I pivoted from my questions of how their programs helped students navigate the education system to ones about broader systems reform. "How does your organization think about changing the systems you and your students operate within?" It's a question they've been asked before. I suspect they most often hear it in their heads, asking themselves why they can't do more to address the root causes of the opportunity gap.

Each of the YDO leaders I spoke with are experienced educators, steeped in the disheartening realities of how schools fail students. Though each YDO leader answered diplomatically, I felt their body language betrayed their frustration at the deep-rooted issues they face. While the navigational approach serves as the starting point for many YDO programs, many have adopted a more transformational perspective. The questions and decisions they face in doing so can be both rewarding and disorienting, but I think deeply powerful.

THE TRANSFORMATIONAL ALTERNATIVE

The navigational approach offers tactical guidance to students but can also risk perpetuating some of the existing barriers and biases of the educational system. The alternative? Some would argue for a more radically transformative approach. If the navigational approach teaches students how to play by the rules, the transformative approach asserts, "The game is bullshit, why can't we change the rules?" As more young voices began to ask this very question, YDOs have begun to reflect on where they see transformative potential in their program approaches.

Dr. Aaliyah El-Amin's work on transformational education for African American youth offered me a helpful entry point in understanding why this approach can be so powerful. In her impactful dissertation, Dr. El-Amin writes that the myth of navigation is "both over-emphasized and misunderstood." She states, "Yes, tools that help African Americans navigate our society are necessary as they give African Americans' resources (education, economic and social capital) to manage racist forces that affect their lives, but they are not enough to address the social practice and order in which racism exists."

El-Amin names that even those African American youth who are able to navigate the most elite educational systems still face racism throughout their adult lives. They've managed to make it through the system, but the system hasn't gotten any better in the meantime. The myth distorts the racism that remains, regardless of one's success. She argues, "To truly remove the burden that African Americans experience as a result of racist forces, we must propose solutions that directly reorganize the social order and disentangle systems and institutions from racist ideologies."

When applied to educational settings, El-Amin argues, we must prepare young people to transform the systems they operate within. In doing so, they will create success for others like them, rather than the touted exemplar who proves the exception to the rule. For educational interventions to truly help minority students, educators have "to shift from a pure focus on helping African Americans navigate society to an equal focus on helping African Americans transform it." (El-Amin, 2015)

Several YDOs are finding ways to integrate a transformative lens into their approaches—some in small ways and some in robust ways. OneGoal, for instance, is committed to training teachers to employ a pedagogy of liberatory consciousness in their approach. While we'll dive deeper into pedagogy in Chapter 10, the way OneGoal leader Nicole Petraglia describes this approach says a lot about the questions they're asking themselves as an organization. Petraglia explains that they want to prepare teachers to not tip the scales towards any one path or future for students. When she first joined the OneGoal team, their primary goal for all students was college graduation. She found herself encouraging students to pursue college far from home, because that was how she approached college and found it impactful. But Petraglia soon pulled back and recognized that each student needed to tailor their decisions to their own needs, priorities and circumstances.

Today, OneGoal teachers strive to give their students information that empowers them to make the most informed decisions they can. Petraglia described a teacher's approach to their students as "you know what is best for you. We are going to support you no matter what path you decide. As long as you have a plan, and you've thought through hurdles that are going to come up...we will support you."

A doggedly transformational approach isn't without its difficulties either. For OneGoal, Petraglia admitted it can be challenging to balance sharing as much information with students as possible while continuing to keep them motivated. She shared an example of how students are prepared for the SATs. OneGoal teachers introduce the SATs in the context of their racist history and introduce the phenomenon of stereotype threat that we discussed in Chapter 4. While OneGoal teachers acknowledge this troubling history, they also acknowledge that most colleges (until this year) required standardized test scores and weighted them heavily in their admissions criteria. It can be overwhelming and demotivating for a teenager who knows this major milestone—getting into college—will be influenced by an unfair test. Though they've committed themselves to empowering their students with maximum information, OneGoal and other transformational YDOs face a challenging decision of just how much of the honest truth of our broken system they should expose.

THE MESSY MIDDLE

While some YDOs favor a narrowly defined approach that's strictly navigational or transformational, most end up in what I call the messy middle. They want to equip students with navigational skills as well as encourage them, where appropriate, to seek change in the systems that don't work for them. In the wake of summer 2020 and the powerful protests of the Black Lives Matter movement, YDO leaders are more attuned than ever to the need to make more lasting systemic change.

At A Better Chance (ABC), they're making some intentional efforts to address identity and systemic issues students may face. Leader Ben Bingman-Tennant shares that they prompt students to consider what it might be like to be the only Black person in class or how people in their new schools may act differently toward them. As Bingman-Tennant explains, "What I'm trying to do is do it in a way that meets them where they are." But he acknowledges that there's room to improve. As an organization that places middle schoolers in prestigious high schools, Bingman-Tennant believes they could do more to support students once they're in their new schools. Their team is actively asking themselves, "How are we building in touchpoints for students as they matriculate and after their first semester of their ninth-grade year? How are we engaging them to try to have those conversations again?"

Although they are in different schools around the country, ABC students have shared experiences, and Bingman-Tennant wants to create space for them to "process together as a community, [to share] what they've learned and what they're thinking about now that they're in those new environments." These are small but important steps. Even these changes to the program, though, are intended to equip students with further knowledge and awareness to navigate sometimes challenging school environments, rather than transform them.

High Jump Campus Director Karen Thomas noted that although she joined the organization with more of a transformation mindset, she quickly adjusted to the reality that High Jump's core program is focused on navigation. "We're more of a band-aid to help get [students] through and open up opportunities," Thomas explains. She notes that part of the balance needed is driven by the families they serve. Thomas draws a difference between many immigrant families and multi-generational families, namely African American families, who have experienced generational trauma in the US. These varied experiences inform how families understand the role of a program like High Jump.

Thomas describes these varied dynamics as a fragile duality; when approaching students, she described thinking that "[W]e want you to be change makers but we also understand that this is your family's chance." The pressure to create upward mobility for their children might lead many families to focus on building navigational skills, rather than rocking the boat and risking life-changing advancement for their family. That said, Thomas fully credits High Jump for being an inclusive space. She agrees that High Jump is intentional about "instilling the awareness" of systemic barriers and equipping students with "the tools for them to be able to survive it." From there, she hopes, students "can figure out how they want to use their education moving forward." In this way, High Jump models how a navigational approach can still integrate identity-based development and active conversation on how identity influences students' paths.

Another YDO, Reality Changers, fully understands the power of their position and the opportunity they have to create young change agents. A justification I've heard throughout my career for not taking a stand on issues is that an organization isn't classified as an advocacy or political organization;

this same rationale arose in some of my YDO interviews. Reality Changers' Director of Programs Jordan Harrison surprised me when, after acknowledging that Reality Changers also is not an advocacy organization, he said that "we want our students to be the folks that are leading the causes for social justice." Though Harrison shared that they're "setting up our students to do so by being more informed about the things of the world," he admits it was a journey to get there.

Part of that journey required Harrison to demonstrate how focusing on transformation would not come at the expense of also preparing students with navigational skills. One great example of this is Reality Changers' revised approach to community service. Previously, Reality Changers students were expected to participate in community service, but they'd usually do so in a shallow way; large groups of students would be organized to help out at a charity walk or other event. Now, students are asked to pick an issue they care about, analyze it, and find a way to serve the community to try and tackle their chosen issue. The activity allows students to still get community service experience, while building new skills and benefits for their college resume. But in the new format, students are also building longer lasting critical lenses in exploring an important issue impacting their community. This offers both a more compelling narrative to use in college or job applications, but more importantly can help transform the systems they operate in.

TAKEAWAYS

The Reality Changers example above is key in considering the tension between navigation and transformation. Positioning them against one another is actually misleading. The two approaches operate in parallel and both are of great value. In systems that routinely deny marginalized students opportunities, it is critically important to know how to beat the system, to "play the game." Parents especially will pressure YDOs to make sure that they deliver on unlocking opportunities by preparing students with those navigational skills. But if students can also gain transformational skills along the way, they can make sure other students like them don't have to navigate so perilously.

The tense, shifting body language of my YDO counterparts makes sense when we begin to uncover some of the challenging decisions and dynamics around navigation and transformation. While most YDO leaders understand the need to strike a balance between the two approaches, it can be difficult to do in practice. This chapter has captured some of the broad reckoning around these questions for YDOs, while the following three chapters will zero in on specific choices YDOs need to make in their teaching approach, narratives, and language in the classroom.

CHAPTER 10:

Pedagogy Matters

"Agree or disagree: If I were giving a speech in front of politicians, I would change the style of my hair so that I look more professional." The students pause, as the instructor reads this statement, and then they spread out in the room, along an invisible spectrum of agreement or disagreement with the statement. "So why did you end up where you did?" the instructor asks. One Latina student shares her position—"I'm not going to straighten my curly hair because it's an important part of me." Another respectfully disagrees because his hair style isn't as important to his identity. After a healthy conversation, the teacher continues with another statement: "I would tell a sad story about myself in order to convince someone to support a cause I care about." The students pause, consider their position and find their next spot in the room.

The conversation is not black and white. There is no resolution, no right answer to strive for. Instead, each student is challenged to reflect on what they value and what they're willing to compromise on. It is a compelling lesson structure that Shawon Jackson, a dynamic youth development leader, uses in his YDO, Vocal Justice. This serves as one illuminating example of the ways YDOs can introduce tools to their students in order to prepare them to both navigate and, as they see fit, transform the institutions they'll continue into. There are several important variables that inform the structure and theory behind a YDO's approach. In this chapter, we'll see some of the variables and decision points YDOs face as they undertake this work.

AGE MATTERS

In deciding whether to take a navigational or transformational approach, YDOs must ground themselves in the developmental stage their students are in. Dr. Sara Johnson, a developmental scientist at Tufts University, shared with me that the way certain pedagogies are used can have serious developmental impacts. She notes that many teachers have focused on explaining systemic inequality, which helps students see that "part of the reason why your life is the way it is, is because of things that are larger than yourself, not because of individual failings." But she cautions that if teachers stop the conversation there, it leads to negative developmental outcomes. When students are introduced to systemic barriers but offered no skills or outlets to address them, Johnson explains, then students don't know where to go from there.

To foster better developmental outcomes, Dr. Johnson explains that revealing systemic biases needs to be paired with a strengths-based approach. In doing so, teachers can emphasize the strengths each of the students offer as individuals and the power of their contributions collectively. The messages shift to "yeah, you've had some odds stacked against you, but you've got some good contributions to make. We can work together and change it and you have the ability to do that." Johnson acknowledged that several youth community organizing groups have successfully struck that balance.

Even with this balanced strengths-based approach, though, students' ages still make a big difference. In part, it informs the level of nuance they can absorb and reflect back. As Johnson explains, "[I]deas about fairness and justice are very salient to younger kids and they develop that sense really early." They can engage in learning about fundamental issues like racism, but they'll understand it in a relatively stark way—that something is fair or unfair. Many students will have experienced injustice first-hand. Learning about these unfair practices in the classroom can be very validating. But in the process of boiling down these complex ideas, students lose certain nuance; Johnson explains that some younger students might come to understand racism as "just when a white person is mean to a black person, which doesn't really address that there are reasons why that happens."

Adolescents are better poised to absorb the level of nuance necessary in these conversations. As Johnson explains, as "you get older, you develop more abstract thinking skills and your world gets a little bigger." Adolescents begin to interact with the world outside of the bubble of their home; they feel the realities of their schools, communities, and cities. They pick up on major national events, such as the President belittling people from certain countries and actively discriminating against entire identity groups. This point in their development proves helpful for these conversations. Though it still requires deep trust and well-trained teachers, curricula that offer critical exploration of systems can be very powerful. These differences in younger students and adolescents proves to be an important variable when considering utilizing a transformational approach, as this approach tends to address systemic issues head on.

CULTURALLY-SUSTAINING APPROACHES

One of the YDOs I learned a lot about, High Jump, tries to navigate the balance between navigation and transformation by taking a culturally-sustaining approach to their work. While he can't control the world outside, High Jump Executive Director Nate Pietrini asks his teachers to set an inclusive tone within the classroom. High Jump takes an intentional approach to developing positive racial and ethnic identity within their students. They do so through an approach of Mirrors and Windows. Through this approach, students are prompted to reflect on their own story and identity and learn about the commonalities and differences of people who are different from them. They have a mirror for themselves and a window into other peoples' lives. "We do our best to ensure that every kid sees themselves reflected in the texts and histories we teach," Pietrini explains. "Whether as a Black man, as a Latina, as a gay student, we try to ensure that they, through some type of reading or writing, celebrate and be proud of their journey and their culture, and they get a chance to respect and understand that of others."

This teaching method strives to take a culturally sustaining approach, building on Dr. Gloria Ladson-Billings' research. Ladson-Billings drew from her research on identity in the classroom to propose the groundbreaking concept of culturally responsive pedagogy, which argued for greater social consciousness, reflection, and analysis in the classroom. Culturally sustaining approaches build upon this idea, by affirming and featuring students' own culture in the classroom. In this approach, students are seen as subjects of the teaching, rather than objects; they gain agency and a say in their teaching, shaping the content firsthand.

These approaches are notably in opposition to deficit approaches. Ladson-Billings started her research by wanting to find a solution to the ways teachers saw African American students as having deficits to overcome, rather than untapped strengths and worth. Since then, many researchers have built on her work, and she too came to support the "remix" of her pedagogical approach—a culturally sustaining model. One common example of this is the incorporation of hip-hop and spoken word poetry in classes with many Black students, a tactic Ladson-Billings herself incorporated in one course. (Ladson-Billings, 2014) This approach can be hugely energizing for students who otherwise feel overlooked in traditional classrooms, and YDOs are primed to take advantage of this approach without the constraints of curricular standards.

For teachers, though, conversations around identity, current events, and power dynamics can feel like a minefield, with little room for error and plenty of opportunities to offend or polarize students. High Jump tries to support teachers by giving them the autonomy to pick topics they feel personally connected to and knowledgeable about. Karen Thomas, one of High Jump's campus directors, touts this flexible approach to the curriculum as a real strength. Led by teachers who are energized by the course content, Thomas sees students come to understand "their own identity by looking through someone else's identity and having those kinds of hard conversations with a teacher that understands this and chooses this and wants to talk about it." Couched in a course aimed at building executive functioning skills, High Jump's conversations around identity offer a great example of how to build inclusive youth spaces; doing so effectively taps into the curricular autonomy and motivated student body that YDOs are fortunate to work with.

As a result, the High Jump team believes their students feel more comfortable in the High Jump classroom and can flourish. "I do feel like they are more comfortable than at their home school because our teachers create that comfort," Thomas shares. Developing this sense of positive identity is key to confronting systemic injustice, which High Jump doesn't shy away from discussing. "We want [students] to know that if they go to a predominantly white institution, they're going to be expected to change to a white cultural norm and that is wrong," Pietrini says. "So in order to not have that create more mess and stress on them, where possible we want to build pride in their cultures." He argues that High Jump is the right place to do it because it offers a place of psychological safety to have conversations that might make students feel vulnerable. In this way, High Jump builds confidence to navigate colleges and at the same time confront the barriers students might face.

Yet the comfortable bubble High Jump builds will likely burst as students graduate from the enrichment program. High Jump makes sure students remain supported, through peer groups and alumni mentors who can relate to the challenges students face. They even encourage action groups within the competitive high schools they'll join as a way of channeling their frustrations into concrete change. This might seem minor, but many peer organizations shy away from encouraging anything that could be perceived as "rocking the boat."

Ultimately, Pietrini makes clear, they want their students to be aware of the realities of entering predominantly white institutions like so many of them will attend. He wants to ensure they know how to navigate these institutions and reap the benefits colleges offer. But he also wants them to have the confidence and knowledge to decide for themselves how they want to adapt. He believes that the processes modeled in the High Jump classroom, including reflection and understanding injustice and inequity and the role of identity on one's personal journey, help students make these decisions.

This is a huge service YDOs can offer. Instead of waiting for college to face these uncomfortable questions, YDOs such as High Jump support students to decide when and how they want to adjust to the settings they're entering and when they want to let their unchanged selves shine. To do this requires a somewhat transformational approach, because it requires an acknowledgement of the biases of the system. But it doesn't ignore the needs to navigate these realities when students aren't able to change them.

Even with the preparation High Jump offers, Pietrini admits making these decisions won't be easy. "No matter what [students] choose, either one can be harmful: either giving up a part of yourself to meet a white cultural norm or being willing to take on the impact of not assimilating to white cultural norms." As Dr. Jennifer Morton astutely writes, "The pressure on strivers is not merely to switch how they are acting at work or school, but to do so while knowing that the power dynamics are stacked against them." (pg 76) But with the skills, confidence and continued support of High Jump, Pietrini hopes his students can manage these challenging dynamics.

CHANGING THE GAME

Every YDO I spoke with and have featured throughout the book had notably tempered perspectives on the idea of transformation. All acknowledged it as important and many, as described in Chapter 9, saw a place for it in their organizations. But one person stood out in his insistence that transformation is a non-negotiable in education today. Shawon Jackson, who led the spectrum game above, gave the most full-throated endorsement of building transformational skills in young people. When I asked Jackson what the purpose of education is today, at the highest level, he said that while today many people will focus on the economic opportunity it unlocks, "there needs to be a clear focus, and it should be social justice. Full stop."

Jackson is walking the walk in his unflinching support for education grounded in social justice. He recently launched the organization Vocal Justice, which aims to build these skills in public school teachers across the US. To start, the organization will train teachers with demonstrated interest in and potential to ground their teaching practice in social justice. With time, these teachers will also be able to train their peers in similar practices.

According to Jackson, these efforts will help fill two current gaps. The first is the lack of critical consciousness; as Jackson says "there's little work that's done within school explicitly to help you say okay, how can I understand social injustices that are happening in the world and then how can I change it." The second gap is a lack of communication skills for students. Jackson argues that communications skills are necessary to usher in organizational transformation. If teachers can equip students with those skills, they will have met the social justice mission Jackson sees as core to education.

Jackson's approach is grounded in critical consciousness. Critical consciousness is the ability to identify and resist oppressive forces in society. (Seider et. Al, 2020) To build this kind of consciousness, students need to both learn critical reflection and feel a sense of agency in influencing change. With these in hand, critical consciousness can lead to sociopolitical action.

Educational institutions offer an ideal outlet to build both critical reflection and agency. Skeptics may see these kinds of lessons as an add-on, but Jackson makes clear that learning critical consciousness isn't a bonus. "As you build critical consciousness you get strong academic outcomes," Jackson explains. "As you focus on building your critical consciousness, you're actually developing a lot of the skills that you need to thrive in school and thrive in the workforce. You must be able to critically examine issues around you. You have to be able to research, and understand the root cause of a problem, think analytically about how you're going to solve that problem, collaborate with other people, communicate effectively, have a strategy about how you're going to move forward, and test hypotheses." Though often labeled "soft skills," these skills are powerful for students' educational and professional potential.

This approach to education offers additional benefits to young people. Jackson finds social justice-oriented lessons to be "more engaging for students. It's more relevant to their lives and so if you want to make sure they're going to do well in school, why not give them a topic area that is relevant." This improved engagement and skills development has a particularly strong effect on students who are most often overlooked. "Research shows that as Black students, in particular African American students, build their critical consciousness, they do better in school," Jackson explained. YDOs should pay attention to this growing body of evidence as they continue to evolve their programmatic approaches. Even if not a singular focus, transformative activities built around critical consciousness could amplify the impacts YDOs seek to make.

In many of these conversations focusing on transformational teaching, one caution educators have is that it can place an unfair burden on the very students who are most impacted by systemic barriers. In his work, Jackson acknowledges this possibility; he says, "The way that I have approached it with Vocal Justice is to say that students should do what they feel comfortable doing at the end of the day." In this way, he aligns with High Jump's Nate Pietrini, in wanting to equip students with maximal information to decide for themselves what they'll take on.

That said, Jackson does still believe that to a certain degree those who most need the change will have to be loud advocates for that change. "It's unfair that the system is set up as it is," Jackson admits. "Yes, it's going to be a burden for us because we're fighting an uphill battle, but if we fight that battle, then things will be better for our communities and for the generation that's after us." In the faces of that burden, Jackson tries to remain focused on his motivation for doing the work—to usher in an educational system that works for every student.

TAKEAWAYS

If most YDOs are preparing folks to play the game, Jackson is changing it. His focus on transformation, inspired by important research, has never felt more needed. While I applaud the work of all the colleagues I interviewed, I have a special appreciation for those who want to transform those systems. With that work, perhaps the rules of the game will finally start to shift.

But, as stated in this chapter, YDOs face several challenging decision points in deciding how transformative they can be in their approach. Students' age and developmental status plays a huge part in whether YDOs can introduce realities of social injustice. Similarly, the pedagogical approach YDOs take proves critical. A more culturally sustaining approach to teaching best supports those YDOs who want to take a more transformational approach.

Like the students in Jackson's trainings who had to decide where they fell on certain issues, each YDO must decide where they fall on the navigational-transformational continuum. Where they fall will have significant impacts on their students for years to come. The question remains how those positions might be shifting in the current socio-political environment.

CHAPTER 11:

From Bootstraps to Tightropes: Influential Narratives

The bracelet read "I am the master of my fate, / I am the captain of my soul." It arrived in one of those spam mailers from a non-profit trying to secure my donation with unnecessary swag. I moved to throw it all away, but the quote on the bracelet caught my eye. I'd heard the same line just days before from an alumnus of the academic placement YDO Prep for Prep. The line, this alum explained, came from William Ernest Henley's poem "Invictus," whose title was also the name for Prep for Prep's signature ethics class. (Cunningham, 2020) The quote became a mantra of sorts for the program, one that its leaders often touted in encouraging students.

The quote says so much in so few words. It articulates a clear sense of autonomy; as masters and captains, we each have the agency to determine our life's path. By asserting that, Henley implies that unexpected storms on the journey are the fault of the individual, of the captain, rather than any outside forces. Imagine being a middle schooler learning about ethics, and you're presented with this quote as the guiding principle in a program that's promised a better future for you. How could you not subscribe? Many do.

The narrative Prep for Prep provides to its students is intentional and powerful, albeit flawed (more on that a little later). With their position so close to young people and often with a higher degree of trust than teachers and other school administrators, YDOs have immense powers of influence over the students. The narratives they choose to use must be intentional, as they can directly inform students' hopes, aspirations, anticipations, and challenges. These narratives can also signal and reinforce whether YDOs take a navigational or transformational approach. Making students aware of the realities behind broader educational narratives, and in some cases, the narratives YDOs employ, proves an important part of revealing the hidden curriculum.

THE BOOTSTRAPS TRAP
"We often in the US talk about education as the key to unlocking all of your dreams for the future," explains Dr. Sara Johnson, a developmental scientist at Tufts University. "There's a lot of effort spent on helping kids reimagine their future selves." Given that YDOs do have to convince students and their families that their programs add value, they need to really create appealing narratives. Often, YDO narratives tap into these prevailing ideas of education's potential, rather than its reality.

Embedded within so many of the narratives YDOs and educators use is the age-old American bootstraps narrative. Grounded in a uniquely American obsession with individualism, this narrative insists that any individual can pull themselves up "by their bootstraps" and achieve whatever they dream. The founder of Prep for Prep, Gary Simons, absolutely bought into this perspective and imbued the program with it. He told parents of his students that "[O]ne of the things we're going to be doing is telling your kids every which way from Sunday that they can do it. That whatever obstacles remain, they can overcome them." (Cunningham, 2020) In many ways, his own trajectory had captured some of that spirit. The son of a housepainter and a homemaker, Simons trained as a teacher, and when he saw how overlooked gifted students were in New York City public schools, he made the entrepreneurial move to launch what would eventually become Prep for Prep. (Cunningham, 2020)

Stories of the self-made man are rampant in our culture, and those who adhere to the bootstraps approach point to them frequently. Immigrant communities, the arbiters of the American Dream today, often ascribe to this belief. Hard work will lead to recognition of merit, and so the children of immigrants are often encouraged to work hard to secure a promising future. Dr. Anthony Jack speaks to this in *The Privileged Poor.* One of the students he features, Valeria, speaks about how her fathers' words ring in her ears as she navigates her prestigious university. "My dad would always teach me, 'You don't want to get where you are based on kissing ass, right? You want it based on hard work. It'll take longer, but there's more value to it. You'll feel more proud.'"

This warning from Valeria's father perfectly captures the idea that seeking help is in opposition to using your skill to get ahead. The idea of turning to a professor for help outside of class feels too much like insider trading, evoking images of shady behind-the-scenes political deals. As the son of immigrants, that's certainly the narrative I absorbed. When navigating elite educational institutions, I think I clung to that sense of meritocracy. Even when I'd learned more about how universities worked and viewed those campus resources as something that had been paid for, I bristled at the idea that I needed to tap into the powerful resources at my disposal to perform at my best. In retrospect, many of my closest friends in college tried to articulate why my stubbornness wouldn't help me and why seeking help didn't need to be seen as dirty, but it took me years to recognize that systems in America rarely operate on merit alone.

THE STORY BEYOND MERIT

This realization, that merit alone doesn't drive success, is an essential lesson of the hidden curriculum. The systems at play are not always structured to reward the highest performing or most capable students with the best educational opportunities; instead, those often go to those who can afford it, or at least afford to invest in the areas to help them get there. If this is the case, then students can be misled by narratives that YDOs use.

This is certainly a critique leveled against Prep for Prep's narrative around rugged individualism. Nikole Hannah-Jones, *New York Times* journalist, fears that programs like Prep for Prep obscure the realities of systemic barriers. "They allow us to say, 'If kids really wanted an education, if they wanted to work hard, they could get it. Look at this program! They can apply for this program!'" she said. "And it allows us to sustain all the other inequality and feel okay about it because we've given this very small avenue to this small number of kids who 'wanted it.'" (Cunningham, 2020) Hannah-Jones articulates one of the greatest consequences of the story that organizations like Prep for Prep tell. If a YDO advances the myth that a student's efforts alone result in success, then every student who faces serious educational barriers—economic, racial, or cultural—will feel betrayed by this false narrative.

High Jump's Benjamin Serrano has seen that betrayal first-hand, both as a High Jump student and later as a staff member working with the organization's alumni. He sees schools, parents, and High Jump alike "hammer home this individualistic mission." High Jump is intentional in doing so because they want to build self-efficacy in their students, to build a belief that they belong in the unfamiliar environment of a private high school and later college. For half the students, Serrano explains, the narrative resonates; they buy into the idea that they belong in the schools and that their strong education will unlock future opportunities. Unfortunately, the other half "internalize it, they go through high school and realize that it was all a lie." Serrano sees a stark confrontation with elements of the hidden curriculum as driving these realizations. As a result, High Jump administrators now have the "green light" to address some of the elements of the hidden curriculum before students face them firsthand. Alumni programming also offers an outlet for students to continue reflecting, venting, and troubleshooting the barriers they face throughout their education.

In this way, High Jump has introduced better balance to the narratives they use.

HIDDEN ETHICAL COSTS

The divergence in how we understand education's role is significant. Dr. Jennifer Morton captures this well in her book *Moving Up Without Losing Your Way*. In her opening, she makes the contrast clear: "The thought that your life opportunities will be determined by the accident of birth is diametrically opposed to the idea of equal opportunity at the heart of the American Dream. As a society, we have viewed our educational institutions as the way of equalizing the prospects of those born into disadvantage." (Morton pg 2)

A philosopher by training, Dr. Morton found herself drawn to consistent philosophical challenges that first-generation, low-income, and non-traditional students consistently faced. She calls these students "strivers," and in her book, she builds an argument for why our current understanding and descriptions of education mask important and often painful ethical costs. "The traditional narrative of upward mobility in this country acknowledges the academic and financial hurdles that strivers have to overcome to succeed, but it does not do a good job of preparing students for the economic, psychological, and ethical challenges they will confront," Morton explains. "We rarely tell students that their success may come at the expense of some of the things that they hold most dear—their relationships with family and friends, their connection to their communities, and their sense of who they are and what matters to them." (Morton pg 12)

Morton argues that strivers often uniquely face hardships and sacrifices in their pursuit of education that are ethical, rather than just financial or academic. As strivers often come from more interdependent communities, either culturally or financially, their educational pursuits can add tension to their existing relationships. For example, if a low-income student contributes financially to their family, then they may be expected to maintain that behavior even while in school; if they can't deliver, this adds conflict to their family dynamic. The fact that many students move away from their home communities to pursue a degree also builds tension. Strivers may be intimately involved in caring for a loved one or wrapped up in challenging circumstances of family and friends. Distancing themselves from that can bring guilt to strivers and a sense of abandonment to those who remain behind.

These very real costs for strivers complicate the more simplified belief that educational pursuits and the upward mobility they offer are an unquestionable benefit to young people. As Morton explains, "Not only is a college degree portrayed as worth any cost—whether financial, ethical or both—but students are expected to make herculean efforts to achieve it." (pg 123) Morton notes that the children of immigrants are less surprised by the costs required to achieve their education; the hard work ethos of immigrant communities makes clear that hard work comes with sacrifice and challenge. For many other students, though, the trade-offs they must decide on can feel jarring, hidden beneath the narratives of what they've always heard about a college education.

It can be especially frustrating for marginalized students to have to make these decisions in ways privileged peers don't have to. Morton makes clear that the ethical costs come from asking students "to choose education over other competing goods." (pg 37) For more privileged students, the trade-off could be spending time to study instead of socialize, or spending money on a professional investment instead of a spring break trip. The stakes are much higher for strivers. Their decisions ripple beyond their own lives, often impacting the lives of their families and communities and more heavily influence their futures. As a result, they have a slim margin for error, adding to the pressures they feel. Unfortunately, according to Morton, "Narratives of upward mobility tend to flatten crucial differences in the challenges that various groups of people experience depending on their place in society." (pg 125)

FROM TIGHTROPE TO SIDEWALK

If all of this is true, then YDOs must seriously reflect on and, where appropriate, amend the narratives they use. Reality Changers has been actively doing just that over the last year. The organization's name reveals the narratives they believe in. The name Reality Changers implies that if you participate in our programs, we will be able to change your reality. Their tagline makes this crystal clear: "College changes everything." Recently, though, they've begun to listen to increasing frustrations from alumni who find that college might bring about a few positive changes, but also its fair share of roadblocks. Jordan Harrison, Director of Programming at Reality Changers, acknowledges that they're considering adjusting the tagline to "college *can* change everything."

While they continue to workshop that tagline, Harrison has brought in a much-needed revamp of the theory that underpins Reality Changers' programming approach. The organization's founder, Christopher Yanov, started Reality Changers as a gang prevention effort. To keep young people away from gangs, the program offered a singular focus on education. He described his approach as the "tightrope theory." As Harrison explained it to me, "These students are walking the tightrope of adolescence, and underneath them there are all these fears. If you magnify the fears, they're going to look down, and they're going to fall into them." To keep students from falling off, Reality Changers provides a clear goal to work toward, with their programs as a tool to keep them balanced and focused on getting to the end of that tightrope.

After working at Reality Changers for a few years (and enlisting Yanov as a great mentor), Harrison came to see the tightrope theory "as complete nonsense." He stepped away from the organization to pursue a graduate degree in education and spent much of that time building a case for why that approach wasn't effective. Since returning to the organization, Harrison has revamped the tightrope theory. Now, students learn that they're on that tightrope in the first place because of systemic barriers, and it is important they recognize that position. The goal of the program, though, isn't to tiptoe across the tightrope, but to break down the systemic barriers to broaden the rope into a sidewalk where many folks can move forward, side by side. These adjustments, and the self-awareness that change is needed, are a large part of why I so appreciate the Reality Changers program. Though Harrison acknowledges they have room to continue refining the narrative, they understand that students will benefit from a reorientation to how their educational journeys might unfold.

SYSTEMATIZING THE SYSTEMS VIEW

The tightrope theory is one helpful example of how YDOs are trying to more intentionally integrate a transformative system view into what has tended to be a more navigational narrative. As Dr. Sara Johnson points out, fewer YDOs "focus on the self in relation to society." Those conversations would prompt students to reflect on questions around why they've had different experiences from their peers and the extra steps they may have to take to get to the same end goal. By not addressing some of these systemic questions, Dr. Johnson believes "youth organizations really run the risk of doing some damage because they perpetuate this idea that if you just imagine something different and work really hard, you too can do that."

In smaller, more gradual ways, many of the other YDO leaders I spoke with were trying to incorporate more of a systems view into their narratives. Lena Eberhart, CEO of Let's Get Ready, says their program is very clear to establish that the American educational system is not a meritocracy. In training both their staff and peer coaches, Let's Get Ready is clear in establishing "this is all being done in the context of an inequitable system," and that the students are not there by coincidence, "they're historically underrepresented for real reasons."

At High Jump in Chicago, the team also tries to build these messages in, though they must tread a bit more delicately as they work with middle school students. Campus Director Karen Thomas sees this come up most explicitly during the high school choice process. Chicago's school district has a complex school choice program; High Jump students, with their strong academic records, must consider many options, including potential scholarships to private schools. In supporting students through this process, Thomas explains, "[W]e help them step back from that name that everybody wants to asking, 'What does that really mean for you as a person?', and always include their family in that [conversation]." Looking beyond just the prestige of a school's name, these conversations also prompt students to prepare for the likely experience of being one of the only students of color in a classroom. These conversations are not intended to dissuade students from taking any particular path, but they do aim to better prepare students with some of the criteria that may not seem obvious. In other words, they make explicit the hidden curriculum of the school choice process.

THE POWER OF PEERS

While the language used by leadership and the conversations held are important elements, the most powerful force in shaping the narratives students hold onto are peers. I've touted the power of near peer models a few times in this book, and this is another strength of that approach. Both Eberhardt and Thomas point to their peer support structures as the most powerful elements of their programs. Peers share common ground from the beginning, allowing them to build deeper trust faster. This trust bolsters their credibility, which means they become powerful spokespeople for a YDO. Thomas notes that High Jump teaching assistants (TAs), all alumni of the program who are current high school and college students, are able to go beyond the "political correctness" of staff. The TAs "freely and willingly say, yes this happened to me...they just lay it out and have these conversations with [students] in a guiding way."

For Let's Get Ready, according to Managing Director of Program Design Grace Bianciardi, "those near peers serve as an incredible role model for our students. Our students aren't just getting this information about what to do and these nudges and reminders about what to do, but they have somebody who often has walked in their shoes, come from similar backgrounds, sometimes has had some shared experiences, and has been trained in how to translate their experience to their younger counterpart." By prioritizing the role of near peers, the program keeps student guidance grounded in reality. As Bianciardi explains, from a peer coach perspective, "When I tell you how to talk to a professor, and how to overcome that barrier, I'm talking to you from experience I'm having right now." In both cases, peers are able to offer a counterbalance to whatever lofty language YDOs might use in their narratives. The narratives of peer mentors are grounded in lived experiences and are therefore even more powerful.

TAKEAWAYS

As YDOs pursue their mission to unlock educational opportunities for marginalized youth, they create stories to convince students and their families that investing in this program will pay off. To do so, they might tap into prevailing narratives of individualism and merit. Although those values are important to cultivate in young people, they do not control the entirety of one's path; systemic barriers against people of particular identities are also powerful. If YDOs can better balance their storytelling for the sake of their students, as so many of the featured YDOs above have, they can better prepare students for the realities they may face. It is this, rather than an uncompromising commitment to old-fashioned notions of individual ability, that will ensure students become the masters of their fate and captains of their soul.

CHAPTER 12:

Language as Barrier and Strength

"When did you become such a good bullshitter?"

My Dad caught me dead in my tracks as we were in the midst of one of our classic debates. I was home during a college break, nestled into the leather couch. In the familiarly worn cushions, I settled in for yet another intellectual back and forth with my dad, as we had done throughout my adolescence. I was relatively immune to my dad's barbs, as a tough skin is required for Scottish banter.

I don't remember what we were debating, I felt like I was debating my peers back in one of my political science courses. My newly-honed college instincts kicked in and I countered him as I would a classmate. So, when my dad called me out for bullshitting my way through our debate, I sunk deeper into the couch, stung. Was he right? Was I really speaking differently? Had my time away at an elite university caused me to betray my humble roots?

What I realized in that moment is that I had traveled so deeply into the land of the hidden curriculum, had adapted so thoroughly to the formal language styles expected of me, that I hadn't thought to emerge from it when I left for my holiday break. My family picked up on distinct differences in the way I spoke, the new habits I'd formed, the new interests I'd gained. But I hadn't thought to leave those at the door when I arrived home for the holidays. I failed to code- switch, still speaking as I might in the classroom. To me, it had begun to sound normal, but to my family, it sounded stuffy, pretentious. It sounded like bullshit. And bullshit was not part of the Maguire spirit.

Language is an essential part of our identity and a key signifier of our affinity with family and community. When language shifts, it can feel like one's identity shifts with it. That can feel threatening to those who hold to that identity so dearly. For me, the language shifts were subtle, but nonetheless surprising to my parents. For young people who speak a language other than English at home, or speak with a stronger accent or different dialect, that contrast can be even harder to negotiate.

As a central element of the hidden curriculum, language proves a powerful tool for students to break through the coded classroom. Many YDOs encourage students to consider their language when navigating institutions, while others encourage them to find places where they can speak their most naturally to try to transform those spaces. The process of harnessing traditionally "academic" speech can prove troubling for one's sense of self and identity. YDOs, with an approach grounded in identity, can play an essential role in helping students understand what their personal comfort level is in adapting or resisting these dominant linguistic norms.

CODE SWITCH CONUNDRUMS

When the hidden curriculum is grounded in a largely white and wealthy experience, it includes a way of communicating that is most common in those spaces. For students raised in homes and schools where that is not the dominant way of speaking, they will often see code-switching as an important tool in navigating the hidden curriculum. As Let's Get Ready CEO Lena Eberhart shared, "Kids already know about code-switching...they're so sophisticated at this point about what's required." Adolescent young people of color in particular will likely have confronted linguistic differences in their lives before the college process. Whether interacting with teachers, negotiating neighborhood dynamics, or in the scariest cases, navigating precarious conversations with police, young people of color often come to know the power of code-switching. For Eberhart, she notes that students "teach [teachers] what's required for them to get what they want."

This is certainly the case in educational settings and, in particular, in navigating the college process. This came up for Yasmine during one of her boarding school interviews with

A Better Chance, where she was accompanied by her mom. Afterwards, Yasmine shared, "My mom was making a joke like, 'Wow you really turned into like a whole different person.'" But Yasmine felt that in that moment, that it "wouldn't be okay if I spoke like I was talking to my mom." Although this was likely never stated to her point-blank, Yasmine picked up on private schools' implied preference for their students to speak in "standard" English. To do so, Yasmine felt she had to code-switch from the *patois* she spoke with her mom to an academic English style that would appease her interviewer.

Conversations around code-switching often cleave along questions of authenticity and assimilation. These tensions can be felt very acutely when turning to your community, and in particular, your family. Ben Bingman-Tennant, National Director of Programs at A Better Chance, shared that a lot of his students "felt that it was actually hard to come back home, that there was such a disconnect between, let's call it 'white academia,' and their parents' experiences." He explains that often this disconnect is fueled by frank conversations in college about sexuality, race, and gender that might give students new perspective and language around identity that feels foreign to families. Families may go so far as to accuse students of "rejecting our culture" or fear professors "are poisoning you."

Bingman-Tennant readily acknowledges that when he worked at another academic placement organization, his team didn't prepare students or families about what it means "to return to one's community, and undo the code-switching or undo the rules and play by another set." Though he always made himself available to students to try and process the challenges of coming back home, he recognized that this could be something that students and families could have been made aware of.

Dr. Jennifer Morton writes clearly about these tensions with home communities as a common ethical cost of upward mobility through education. "Strivers might feel pressure to downplay the importance of family or community or to prioritize their educational trajectory over commitments to friends," she writes. Morton is describing a stark contrast that strivers uniquely face, one between pursuing education and maintaining their close ties and often essential support to their families' well-being. These are significant ethical costs that do not get adequate attention. With their closer personal positioning to students than many schools might have, YDOs have an opportunity to dig into these costs with students and provide support and solidarity in how they process them.

These are important reminders that code-switching is a skill, one that can feel morally treacherous and comes with costs. Not code-switching might cost a young person validity in the eyes of their peers or professors who expect particular language to be used in the classroom. At the same time, code-switching might cost students connection with peers from their same identity, who see them as betraying their roots in order to get ahead. As Morton writes, "Strivers feel pressure to adapt to and internalize the cultural expectations of the white middle class in order to successfully navigate those institutions. Some of these expectations are superficial, but some of them concern ways of acting and cultural frameworks that cut closer to strivers' core commitments and values." (pg 77) Language is one of many cultural elements that can feel in jeopardy when confronted with the hidden curriculum, and students will have to make important ethical and tactical decisions around how to approach them.

STRENGTH OF A SWITCH

As Morton tells different strivers' stories, she notes cases where they had to acculturate to the dominant cultural norms of American educational institutions. "This culture places a premium on confidence, assertiveness, and being vocal—skills that, for some readers, will seem universally important," Morton writes. (pg 104) Yet she acknowledges that many other cultures value deference, hierarchy, and listening over speaking. Dr. Morton is appropriately calling out a strong Western bias in academic classrooms, another way the hidden curriculum manifests.

Bingman-Tennant shared one interesting example of this. One of his former students was a refugee from Haiti, who had experienced a great deal of trauma surviving the 2010 earthquake there. He eventually made it to college through the YDO's program but found himself culturally at odds with his classmates. He had been enrolled in a freshman writing seminar about gender and sexuality. In it, he shared his own experience and perspective on gender roles, ones that are quite traditional. His classmates accused him of being a sexist and piled on their critiques, causing him to wonder if he could really make it in an American college.

But when Bingman-Tennant dug into why the student held these views on gender, he shared that these traditional gender roles had been important in surviving the aftermath of the earthquake. From his view, a clear division of labor had proved essential to their survival, so he felt this view held some utility in his life. Admittedly, I would have probably joined the critiques if I were this student's classmate, but the story gives me pause in how Western-centered our educational models can be. In a world with a less dominant, narrow path of classroom participation, this student's perspective could carry equal value with his peers. His contribution could be seen as unique, rather than just at odds with the norms of his peers. It could have been seen as a strength, not a deficit.

Whether a Black student changing their dialect or an immigrant hiding their cultural norms, our education system can create a pressure to assimilate, or else, isolate. As high school teacher Amy Charpentier shared with media outlet Vox, even a single word can knock a student's sense of belonging. She described a bright student of hers who made it to an elite liberal arts university; once there, the student found her peers using the word misogyny in class as if everyone knew what it meant, but she did not. As this student began to question if she could keep up at this school, Charpentier stepped in to say, "You, who doesn't understand the word 'misogyny,' knows two languages, knows how to run a restaurant with your eyes closed, knows how to take care of kids. It's about: How do you find value in the experience you do have?" (Chang, 2018)

Charpentier's words are powerful. The reality is that students' ability to vary their communication style and adapt themselves to many settings is a huge strength. Yasmine had an affirming experience of her own at Wellesley High. In an English class, her teacher assigned a story that used a different dialect, unique to the community of the characters. She remembers her peers complaining, questioning why they were being taught something in "broken English." The moment offered Yasmine the opportunity to speak up, to say she understood it because she had spent her entire life surrounded by Caribbean people speaking in a different dialect. The moment was most powerful, though, because Yasmine picked up on her teacher's intentionality. "She did that for a reason, to say, some people may be able to better understand something, that this is a whole language within itself," Yasmine shared. Her teacher created a space for Yasmine's unique strengths to come through, positioning her as valued, not as an anomaly.

NAVIGATING LINGUISTIC DIFFERENCE

Yasmine's experience is one great example of the ways educators can buffer against the difficult dynamics their students may face as a result of the hidden curriculum. YDOs in particular, with the flexibility their programs offer, can and should do this. But getting to that point can be challenging when an organization tries to strike a balance between a navigational and transformational approach.

High Jump certainly felt that way. As mentioned in Chapter 10, High Jump continues to negotiate this line. They very intentionally ground their teaching in affirming students' identities and don't shy away from some of the hard truths their students face. The organization's Executive Director Nate Pietrini certainly understands how valuable that is. He immediately impressed me with his savviness around identity and equity. He had a particularly clear-eyed response when asked about expectations of students to code-switch:

"Why should our kids, or any kid, have to code-switch? Just acknowledging the need to do so implies that there's a racial hierarchy or a dominant structure and one of those races or cultural groups is right and one of them is wrong. In education, the group—that has set the cultural norms for which code-switching is required where you have to critique your slang, critique your dress—the group who requires that has a history of oppression over the other group, and not only has oppressed them but has actually stolen some of their culture and appropriated some of their culture...I'm not comfortable with the responses that tell the oppressed race to assimilate, to conform, or to reduce it to navigation...we think kids need to understand code-switching, but the fact that they even have to do it, that is unjust."

Pietrini offers a nuanced point of view on code-switching: that it is a tool for navigation, which assumes that there's a narrow path of how to appropriately navigate our institutions. The pressure to code-switch, among other things, signals to young people that the customs, language, and behaviors of their own family, culture, or community do not carry value in this space. Pietrini actively seeks to build a community at High Jump that rejects this notion, and instead employs a strengths-based approach. He described an approach to affirm students' identities by using content of diverse histories and stories, the Mirrors and Windows approach described in Chapter 10.

Alumni I spoke with agreed that in the High Jump classroom they felt affirmed. Jess Mora shared that no matter the assignment, whether a personal essay or a response to a Shakespeare play, "We were always encouraged to find our own voice and find our own way of saying things and expressing ourselves." She felt that the High Jump community reinforced pride in herself. She held firm to her sense of self even when she was "in these spaces that have these different norms, that make you feel like you might need to fit in." Jess's experience with High Jump resonated in what I heard from other alumni.

While the High Jump experience is affirming, students still struggle in navigating the realities of the elite schools they graduate into. Alexa Ramirez, who also found great affirmation in the High Jump community, understands some of the limitations of taking a more transformative approach. As a current college student, Alexa realized that "never again will I have the opportunity to be in a classroom in which I can just talk to people who literally go through the same thing… where we don't have to explain our humanity to each other." Alexa clearly felt comfortable with her peers, speaking openly and naturally.

She noted, though, that there is such a thing as too much awareness of the hard truths when you're a middle schooler. Though she can tangibly recognize the ways High Jump helped her life, the journey was a struggle. She and her fellow High Jump alumni friends recently reflected on the question: If we knew all the challenges we would face, would we still say yes to High Jump? The answer: "We don't know if we would do that again."

TAKEAWAYS

Although most students who must do so are quite familiar with code-switching, the linguistic gymnastics students face in school can be challenging and draining. YDOs can offer an outlet where that's less necessary, where students can speak in their most comfortable way. YDOs must be intentional about creating that space. Doing so contributes to affirming the language and experience of students as a strength, rather than a deficit to be corrected and switched out of. YDOs can also help students prepare for and process the transitions between college, family, and other communities. In doing so, they can help avoid frustrations and, perhaps even accusations of, bullshit. Students' perspectives on language in education will inform how they navigate institutions and their relative comfort in transforming these institutions. In this way, an explicit acknowledgement of the power of language and an opportunity to decide how to approach one's language prove powerful in combatting the hidden curriculum.

CHAPTER 13

Facing the "In-Our-Face Challenges"

In 2004, renowned education leader Peter Edelman wrote a compelling call to action for practitioners in his field. He observed, "I don't see great emphasis in the literature, or more important, in much of the practice, on taking on the racism and the economic stratification and the lousy schools and the recalcitrant employers and the awful juvenile and criminal justice and child welfare systems, and all the rest of it. But maybe the point of youth development work is to be the infantry, the people on the front line who do the one-on-one work that is a vital part of the answer, and maybe the only one that works in an immediate sense. Maybe taking on the big stuff is somebody else's responsibility." The image of the youth development staff member as a frontline worker certainly resonates, particularly amidst the COVID-19 pandemic when this book was written, when we've come to acutely feel the influence of educators on young people.

And yet, Edelman does not rest at the individual, frontline work. "I keep thinking that more is possible—that, even with the fact that there are only twenty-four hours in the day, youth development as a field could encompass more explicitly attention to and connection to fighting against the larger force that are stacking the deck against too many young people in America." Edelman writes, "Heaven knows, we need it. The people in Washington are openly and ostentatiously cutting taxes to make the rich richer and to make it impossible for our country to find the money to do something about the long list of real national needs that we have. We need—desperately need—people, especially young people, to take up the in-our-face challenge that has been placed before us. There's nothing secret going on here, no backroom deals, no silent coup. The whole thing is right there—blatant, unmistakable." I shivered when I read this passage. I was struck by how perfectly his description applied seventeen years later of daunting countercurrents, gridlocked politics, and shameless ignorance of obvious inequities.

Throughout this book, I've uncovered some of the common ways the hidden curriculum manifests, the ways youth development organizations teach, translate, and shape that hidden curriculum, and the complex dynamics and decisions YDOs make in that work. Though there is great value in naming these dynamics, I couldn't help but yearn in my interviews for a productive outlet, a future facing 'so what.' Everyone I spoke with readily acknowledged the brokenness of the systems they operated within, but few functioned with a formal mandate to try and make it less broken. I couldn't help but wonder if YDOs occupy an influential position for changing the lives of individual students, then what could that mean about changing the system? Could more YDOs place more energy behind systemic change rather than just individual change, and if so, should they? Could YDOs go beyond a transformative approach to their teaching and take direct action in transforming systems to be more inclusive?

MEETING THE MOMENT

There's no doubt that students' perspectives on the systems they exist within are changing. As our country continues to more intentionally and publicly reckon with our racist past and present, young people are holding the old guard accountable. If students' academic outlooks or leadership opportunities shifted, YDOs would adjust; so, when the sociopolitical landscape evolves, shouldn't YDOs?

One force that's demanding answers to these questions is the Black At movement. This phenomenon has seen Black students past and present come together online to share stories of their negative experiences in different schools. These have been particularly stark at elite private schools, including schools that some YDOs partner with. Let's take the BlackAtExeter Instagram account, which captures the experiences of Black students at the Ivy League-feeder boarding school Phillips Exeter Academy. One student shared that one of his first nights in his dorm, he walked into the room and another student joked, "Oh you're here, it's time to play ghetto music." No one spoke up to call out the racist behavior, and this student was left worrying that he'd be living with this kind of racism for the next four years.

In other cases, students were told by faculty and advisors that they couldn't possibly succeed in certain classes or get into their dream colleges. One student powerfully captured so many of the dynamics I've discussed here. She shares, "At the beginning of my Prep year, I told a white girl that I liked her sweater and asked where it was from. She didn't say anything, looked at me like I was stupid, and just pointed to the alligator logo on it. I felt incredibly humiliated...it marked the tone of my time at Exeter—an outsider unable to understand the code." The offending student assumed that her peers had the cultural capital to recognize a Lactose logo, a luxury brand accessible to few. Her response to someone who didn't shows the nasty underbelly of racist student cultures at these elite schools.

Like Exeter, Black At accounts have sprung up at almost every major prestigious high school and university. YDOs, too, have had accounts made about their own programs or were made aware of the accounts related to schools they work with. Ben Bingman-Tennant at A Better Chance readily acknowledges that the Black At movement has generated important conversations for their organization. His team is trying to figure out how best to support their students in pushing for more inclusive institutions. He recognizes that the students they're placing in these kinds of schools are young people "who can have those conversations and force institutions to rethink themselves in ways that are important for us."

Broadly, YDOs understand that students are generally more tapped into systemic issues and their own identities. Benjamin Serrano at High Jump noted at a recent reunion of program alumni, one student readily shared her experience about a protest she was helping to organize. Serrano was especially struck by the timing; "This is in October, just two months into high school, and she was already doing that. I hadn't seen it before. So, I think that's definitely changing," Serrano shared. He hopes that at least some of this is a result of strong identity formation and affirmation at High Jump. "Our students are better critical thinkers than what they used to be," Serrano shares. "I think that's because certain aspects of the program are teaching them more and more about the world and their identity."

TURNING THE CRITICAL LENS INWARD
With more vocal students, it's inevitable that the same critical lens they bring to their schools will also be turned on the YDOs themselves. For one, students fundamentally feel the unfairness of the system when they see their peers not get the same opportunities as they get. Students across YDOs recognize over time that they've uniquely unlocked opportunities in spite of the system, not because the system has gotten better. Students at SEO, like Alexander Rodriguez, feel "it's 'devastating' to consider the reality that there are students outside of the program being left behind." (Swaak, 2020) Essentially every student has friends from their schools who tried unsuccessfully to get into SEO, and participating students see firsthand the different trajectories that lead to inclusion in the program This proves to be a common tension YDOs face—striking a balance between helping many students succeed broadly or providing really deep support to fewer students.

Part of this tense dynamic is that SEO is already focusing on the students who excel. Millie Hau, SEO's vice president for high school programming, describes their average student as one that "might not have been identified in ninth grade for certain advanced classes,[but] they're not in danger of dropping out, so they're just in the middle, being undereducated." (Swaak, 2020) This reality means that while a program like SEO Scholars can improve the lives of individual students, it can't radically change the system, at least not on its own.

Students are increasingly willing to put YDOs on blast for perpetuating some of the very barriers they claim to work against. At an annual gala for the academic placement organization Prep for Prep, a young alumnus called out the organization's leadership. "I want to know," he began, "whether you feel that there needs to be an ideological shift from a white-supremacist, elitist mentality that Prep is at minimum participating in, if not encouraging or propagating." The crowd quieted, and he went on. Many of the Prep kids he knew and had mentored had a "fraught relationship" with this "Prep identity," he said, "given Prep's relationship with white-supremacy norms." (Cunningham, 2020) This is an astounding and important call-out for one of the most frequently critiqued YDOs operating today. It's also a sign that in the most public of forums, YDO leaders need to be prepared for challenges from students and calls for greater accountability.

Alexa Ramirez, the High Jump alum, confronted the dark side of the ecosystem in which non-profits like High Jump operate within. Every year, Alexa explained, High Jump holds a fundraising gala and invites a few High Jump alumni to join. "I remember I'd be so so jealous that I didn't get invited," she admits, but she was finally invited her senior year of high school. By that point she and her friends were "the backbone of activism at my high school," and primed to pick up on power dynamics. So, when she was asked to walk around the room during an auction to record donor's bidding numbers, she was struck by feeling "like a trophy, like an object." Alexa looked at these mega-rich white people treating this as a game, when, in reality, she felt they "shouldn't even have this money...this generational wealth was built on slavery." She felt it was absurd that High Jump was "begging for this money" and flaunting their students as carrots in a bidding war. After years of feeling accepted by High Jump, Alexa became disillusioned with the organization for the first time. As she made clear, the principles on which High Jump was built are inherently biased.

Many of the YDO administrators I spoke with are in touch with these dynamics and recognize the very real tradeoffs they face in courting donor money. Some of the organizations have rethought their approach to fundraising, as many alumni of these programs have leveled critiques around the tokenization and trotting out of young, predominantly students of color at galas and other events. Others have had to grapple with potentially losing donor dollars by taking a public stance on social issues.

Reality Changers faced exactly that challenge. Jordan Harrison shared "we as an organization made statements on Black Lives Matter and DACA. And a few of our donors said, 'Hey, I don't support these things,' and just completely pulled out." This is one of worst-case consequences of speaking out, but Harrison stands by the decision wholeheartedly. After important internal discussions, the team concluded that "we can't honestly say that we're going to support our students and be silent on issues that are going to crush their lives." I can't help but feel that Reality Changers is particularly committed to taking these public stances in part because the students they serve are not necessarily the high-performing students that are often served by other YDOs. The Reality Changers team knows that their students would otherwise get left behind and even with Reality Changers' help, they will still face many battles in a society structured against them. With this backdrop in mind, I view Reality Changers' public position as especially courageous.

As YDOs try to take a stand despite donor constraints, though, they're also being asked to do more and more. The goalposts keep shifting. As Lena Eberhart said, "The list of responsibilities keeps getting longer and longer." She flags that Let's Get Ready started out as an SAT prep organization but expanded to college guidance and retention because they continued to identify new and greater student needs. Today, they are expanding even further to include career services and professional opportunities. Fundamentally, according to Eberhart, "the problem is that we have to keep training these kids how to be different to fit in... There's something off big time." In my eyes, this constant broadening of the YDO reach is indicative of a larger problem: that the formal education system can't serve the students in the way they need it to. For YDO administrators like Eberhart, they can't help but wonder, "[W]hy is it that youth development organizations are the people who are dealing with this and what is our role in potential reform?"

HARNESSING THE COLLECTIVE POWER OF YDOS

If all of this is true—that students are increasingly insisting on more change and YDOs recognize the need—then how might YDOs go about achieving that change? In almost every case, these organizations are structured to support the individual. Yet their mandate exists because of gaps in the system. The administrators I spoke with all vigorously agreed that the system was broken. But they were also largely quick to acknowledge that it wasn't necessarily their scope to try and fix it. YDOs largely are not positioned to do so effectively.

This makes sense as individual entities, but when you consider the networked influence of so many like-minded and like-missioned organizations, there could be immense collective impact. Some sophisticated funders have begun to recognize that. Though Lena warned that many donors advocate for mergers and acquisitions in the field, some are trying to bring "together their grantees to share best practices or try to learn from each other in a non-competitive environment." And yet, according to Ben Bingman-Tennant, even low-stakes efforts to bring YDO practitioners together easily fall apart. Bingman-Tennant spoke of a recent call he joined with peer organizations, one of whom was trying to start a data collection initiative across peers. Unfortunately, "about five minutes into the call, it sort of disintegrated because no one would agree on what data to collect, no one would agree on the outcomes, or how the data would be used." Bingman-Tennant lamented that even in the moments of the most obvious alignment, YDOs "don't always see through their differences and find the common ground," his own organization included.

Despite these obvious roadblocks, I couldn't shake the feeling that collectively, a network of YDOs could be uniquely influential. When I asked about existing networks, colleagues shared several interesting resources. One great example is NCAN, the National College Attainment Network. This association brings together a wide cross-section of stakeholders, from donors and universities to many non-profits and community organizations like the YDOs featured here. Their mandate is broad, driving interesting research and resources to improve college attainment; that includes a major focus on financial access and a focused push to improve FAFSA completion in college applicants. A similarly structured organization, the National Association for College Admissions Counseling, or NACAC, also brings together educational institutions, community organizations, and independent advisors to share best practices in advising students on postsecondary educational opportunities. These organizations, and many others, offer a national, expansive network of stakeholders that can support one another.

These organizations do not exclusively focus on the needs and dynamics of youth development organizations working outside of, but often in partnership with, formal educational institutions. A few organizations have tried to narrow their focus on youth organizations. For instance, the Student Success Network (SSN) supports educators in providing greater socio-emotional learning opportunities for their students. This network's membership reflects the rich diversity of the youth development sector, with members including OneGoal, SEO, and Let's Get Ready. SSN provides important capacity building to members to provide quality programming on a topic that's overlooked by many formal educational institutions. In New York City specifically, the Youth Development Institute supports youth-serving organizations in the city with a focus on positive youth development. These are two of the few examples YDOs leaders could point to as associations serving youth organizations specifically.

Like the YDOs, these associations do some important work and there's no doubt their resources prove a boon to YDO partners. But none exclusively organize youth development organizations around the unique challenges they face. Colleges have a wide number of lobbying and networking outlets, as do specific kinds of schools' administrators. But I have yet to find an organization that harnesses the incredible energy and vast reach of YDOs across the country. It feels like a missed opportunity.

As I spoke to YDO administrators from Chicago to New York, San Diego to Atlanta, I couldn't help but feel that they all were speaking one another's language, that they shared so many frustrations and barriers. The students YDOs serve share similar concerns, whether disinvestment from their communities, under-resourced schools, inaccessible college applications and financial aid processes, and unwelcoming college environments. YDOs are uniquely positioned to understand and amplify their students' stories, to make human the impacts of what can sound like theoretical challenges. Together, a network of YDOs could also lobby their partners and donors to work collaboratively to improve the systems they work within. When the silos break down, funders might be more likely to support longer-term, structural projects in addition to the day-to-day service provision YDOs already offer.

Most excitingly, a YDO lobbying network could offer an outlet for students to make their own voices heard. There are several incredible youth advocacy groups to take inspiration from, including Young Invincibles, which has been a leading voice in reforming the FAFSA form, and DegreesNYC, which is pressuring the New York City government to commit to close the gap of college enrollment and graduation rates for low-income students and students of color. Having spoken to just a handful of exceptional YDO alumni, I know how convincing and powerful their own narratives and energy could be in ushering in real change. They've certainly influenced me in meaningful ways, and I would love to see that energy harnessed for more systemic reform.

TAKEAWAYS

YDOs have always been part of a broader, broken education system. With that, they sometimes perpetuate some of the same harms they're trying to help students overcome. Since the murder of George Floyd, YDOs have joined the country in a reckoning of their complicity in perpetuating racism and other biases. Students are increasingly holding them accountable to do better. YDO leaders know and appreciate this and yearn to see the systems change that is so needed. Together, they could harness their collective voice to fight for those changes, but right now that opportunity is largely missed.

I hope that upon reading this, someone will reach out to me and tell me I've egregiously overlooked an organization that does just that. But until then, I'll daydream of the day when YDOs come together and unite not only to share best practices, but also to push for systemic changes to help their students achieve their greatest dreams. I'll leave you with the closing remarks from Peter Edelman, which feel as relevant a call to action today as they were seventeen years ago: "My purpose is to challenge all of us to step up our game, and, even more important, to challenge all of the young people with whom we work to play to the hilt their role as citizens and participants in the American community. That, in the end, is the only way we're going to have even a fair shot at making youth development into the force that it ought to be in fulfilling America's promise."

Conclusion

YDOs are shape shifters, serving in many nuanced roles for both young people and the education system broadly.

YDOs are decoders. They decode the hidden curriculum that's subtly etched between the lines of formal curricula, course guides, and financial aid forms. YDOs help decode the foreign dynamics of wealth, whiteness, and privilege that might be startling for students to confront in college. They serve an essential role in helping students make sense of the labyrinth of new realities and hopefully equip students with the skills to manage college on their own when needed.

YDOs are translators. They interpret complex processes, policies, and practices and rework them to be more digestible and accessible. YDOs can translate the opaque college admissions and financial aid processes and make sense of academic lingo and overly formal jargon. Students turn to them in trying to understand the behaviors of their peers, and hopefully feel more confident in facing school.

YDOS are cheerleaders. They build enthusiasm by creating college-going cultures, with encouraging (albeit sometimes misleading) narratives of what could be in students' futures. They foster self-efficacy in students, instilling that fundamental belief and skill that seeking help and leaning on available resources can be powerful. YDOs instill a balanced perspective that students can have hope for their future prospects despite the systemic barriers they face.

YDOs are bridges. They offer a pathway from underinvested schools and communities to some of the most competitive high schools and colleges, in turn unlocking promising career and financial prospects. Sometimes that bridge is the direct work of an academic placement YDO, and in other cases, the YDO offers the skills and supplemental teaching to break into these elite institutions. They bridge an education system that fails so many students.

But YDOs are merely a band-aid. For all the amazing work they do, YDOs can only patch over the systemic failures that cut so deeply in many low-income communities and communities of color. With rare exceptions, their work focuses on helping individual students navigate through the system despite the barriers they face, rather than remove the barriers firsthand.

Five powerful metaphors that reflect just some of the many roles YDOs occupy. These metaphors speak to the incredible role YDOs play in the lives of young people. They speak to the inequalities YDOs work to overcome, and they acknowledge the shortcomings YDOs face in trying to undo systemic barriers. If we were to overlay these metaphors atop one another, we would get a messy picture and that seems like a fitting point on which to end. YDOs are vital and yet limited, energizing and essential even if hamstrung. In a broken system, they teach between the lines so that young people don't get lost there.

FINAL TAKEAWAYS

The hidden curriculum is powerful and underestimated. Although some colleges and educators are becoming savvy to it, the hidden curriculum must be made explicit. Once out in the open, it will hold less power.

YDOs serve as an essential player in doing just that. In their close relationships with students who are most marginalized, YDOs are able to teach, translate and decode the elements of the hidden curriculum that students will inevitably confront in their college journeys. They take different approaches to this work, from placing students in top performing schools to preparing them with academic and life skills to thrive in these settings.

YDOs help students navigate the hidden curriculum by creating an inclusive college-bound culture to energize them. They help students understand the unfair and complex college admissions system and prepare them for the unstated academic and social dynamics of elite universities. YDOs cultivate a strong sense of self-efficacy in students, to help them tackle the likely challenges they'll face despite the added preparation.

Throughout their work, YDOs face a series of challenging decisions points. These moments force YDO leaders to consider how much they invest in helping individual students to navigate the educational system and how much they work to transform the education system into a more inclusive system from the start. This tension informs YDOs' pedagogical approach, organizational narrative and approach to language. I see great potential in the opportunities for YDOs to coalesce around a united voice to lobby for needed systemic change and I look forward to cheering on their work.

To my readers: If you're a community member, I hope you'll walk away with a deep appreciation for the essential, life-changing role youth development organizations play. If you represent a youth development organization, I hope you feel affirmed in your work and challenged to reflect on the potential of systemic change in the field's future. And if you're a student navigating high school and college today, I hope you've gained some insight into the hidden curriculum to help you prepare for your college journey. I hope this book has offered a space for reflection and analysis, made you frustrated and energized to unlock opportunities for young people who so deserve it. Ultimately, I hope I've illuminated the power of teaching between the lines.

Epilogue

This book has been an incredible personal journey for me. When I started writing this book, I intended to approach it more as a journalist. I felt at times like I needed to check my own preferences at the door, to avoid making my book a "how to" on effective youth development. Instead, I led with the voices of experts in the field and young people, to illustrate both the opportunities and challenges in the sector.

But I can't ignore that I began writing this book in the summer of 2020, delving into my research at the height of nationwide Black Lives Matter demonstrations. As calls rang out for deeper, systemic change, I saw this book as an opportunity, in my own corner of the country, to argue for that change.

With this in mind, I've written and featured the work of several amazing youth development organizations. Each of them should be commended on their important work. Each organization has clearly impacted the individuals they reach in a way that often significantly changes the course of their lives. As I interviewed YDO administrators, alumni, and researchers, I couldn't help but feel that the impact on individual lives was no longer enough, and frankly, never was.

Though I had been increasingly agitated by the incremental change I witnessed in my day-to-day work with young people globally, the protests for Black Lives in 2020 tipped the scales for me. Systems reform needs to happen; to make and sustain that change, young people need to be equipped with the skills to do so if they choose. With constrained curricula, schools will likely move slowly on this. YDOs, on the other hand, have a greater opportunity for substantive change. YDOs are situated directly in the middle of so many systemic inequities; the students they support are those who will be most harmed by unfair structures. Assuming that individual impacts add up to systemic change is not enough. YDOs have a responsibility to reckon with these dynamics head on and decide intentionally how to address them in their programs, if at all.

I won't go so far as to say that the YDOs that choose to continue avoiding systemic change are doing harm. As long as they continue to influence individuals who most need the support, they are bridging notable gaps in educational opportunity. But they will have also missed an incredible opportunity to right the wrongs they claim to want to fix. History has consistently favored those pushing for more inclusive institutions and I have to believe that the same will be true in this moment.

I started writing this book with the intention of revealing two hidden phenomena: 1) the presence of the hidden curriculum, those powerful but unstated norms, behaviors, and language in the American education system; and 2) the unacknowledged role that youth development organizations play in teaching, translating, and shaping the hidden curriculum for the students least likely to learn it on their own. Acknowledging the presence of both of these elements allows us to then respond to both more intentionally.

Intentionality proved to become the underpinning of my research. For one, I wanted to see an intentional acknowledgement of the powerful role I witnessed YDOs playing. I wanted to recognize the challenging dynamics they operate within and the decisions, passive and active, they have had to make. In turn, I also found myself desiring greater intentionality on the part of YDOs. As I've noted frequently throughout this book, the work of each YDO featured is impactful and important. YDOs face endless asks with limited resources. The invisible burden this work of the hidden curriculum places on YDOs sometimes means that the work isn't addressed head-on; when it's not a stated part of the organization's mandate, how can they ensure the work is completed with the same intentionality as other program elements? I believe that these two intentions are inextricably linked, that if communities can acknowledge the importance of this work, then YDOs can hold themselves to greater accountability in addressing the dynamics of the hidden curriculum in the best possible way. I hope my book helps generate greater acknowledgement and, in turn, greater intentionality.

With this in mind, I hope you, reader, will have used this book as an opportunity to reflect on how much systemic change you want to see. As a former student, did you take for granted the ease with which you navigated a system of higher education? If you work in YDOs, where do you want to see your organization stand on these questions? If you are an educator in formal institutions, how do questions of the hidden curriculum apply in your setting as well? How can you better support those organizations pushing for more radical reform? If you are a student, what kind of world do you want to live in, and how are the organizations you turn to for support helping to shape that world? These might sound like pie-in-the-sky questions, but I mean them as reflections on the tangible, small steps we can each take on the spheres we influence.

I pose these questions to you because I've had to start confronting many of them myself. This process unearthed biases I held. I've been challenged on my understanding of dialectal difference, of the power of linguistic diversity. I've changed my mind on methods to approach youth development, cautioned against projecting a singular, narrow pathway of success and instead broadening the process to allow unique individual strengths to shine. I've realized that language and narratives I use are often grounded in deficit-based rather than asset-based framing and the consequences of those subtle word choices. I've probably made some mistakes still in writing this book and have no doubt that, in the same way I've learned from so many of the folks I interviewed for this book, I will continue to learn from incredible leaders.

Ultimately, I've been inspired, most notably by the outstanding young people I spoke with fighting for change in big and small ways. Their commitment to liberation lifts me, calls me to do more. I hope this book contributes to that effort and serves as a seed of continued growth, inclusion, and equity.

Acknowledgements

When I started this writing journey, I had no idea where this would take me. But no surprise, like so many of the things I take on, I had to lean on my community to get me through it.

To Eric Koester, Brian Bies, and the entire New Degree Press team—thank you for creating an accessible community to tell stories that would otherwise remain untold. To my editors, Paloma Wrisley, Gina Champagne, and Kathy Wood—thank you for your accountability, patience, and genuine enthusiasm for this project.

This book is the product of a lot of talking out loud, hand-wringing, and second-guessing. To the many folks on the other end of those conversations, thank you. My appreciation to Christian Tanja, Roya Zahed, Surabhi Lal, and Mark and Clare Overmann for your patience in the earliest conversations as I brainstormed where this book might be going. A special shout-out to some incredible friends who stepped up as readers of early drafts: Ryan Derby-Talbot, Olivia Route, John Phillips, Sarah Sagan, Kelsey Harpham, and Roya Zahed. You went above and beyond, giving me the real-talk feedback I needed to make this book as impactful as possible.

I trusted in my tribe to buy into this effort, literally, and buy you did. To my pre-sale backers, thank you. You allowed this book to become a reality and get in the hands of those that can hopefully be positively influenced by it. Thanks to: Rob Holland, Chris Caines, Kyle Ogilve, Sara Mason, Brad Watt, John Phillips, Kelsey Harpham, Mum & Dad, Casey Herrick, Annie Route, Roya Zahed, Mischa Noll, Becca Wadness, Sarah Sagan, Nick Armstrong, Brian Alosco, Kyle Witzigman, Sarah Bleiberg, Courtney Chaloff, Deanna Wertheimer, Priscilla Suero, Lori Murphy, Maddie Rita, Marissa Wainwright, Craig Maguire and Jacqueline Vaughn, Veronica Venezia, Jayme Wiebold, Patrick Hackett, Mathew Shepard, Ali Thomas, Allanah Rolph, Shannon Moselle, Nick Tseng, Vincent Pham, Joyce Chiao, Sebastian Dziallas, Devon Kuehne, Anjali Jacob, Sarah Sklar, Shelley Hoy, Eric Koester, Moire Corcoran, Sloane Speakman, Lucy Grierson Bertsch, Chelsea Fricke, Matthew Kastellec, Sothdra Nguon-Devereaux, Clay McKeon, Claire Kelly, Adam Meyer, Rishi Ahuja, Ryan Derby-Talbot, Lisa George, Amy Burns, Shelley Effman, Amber Hill, Leslie Alvarez, Liz Zechmeister, Tala Mansi, Loan Kim Chu, Eri Okuma, Anna Fireman, Wendy Miller, John Gershman, Nguyen Huu Diem Huong, Sabra Drummond, KinHo Chan, Peter Peltack, Caroline Martin, Jackson Nguyen, Ian Frazier, Hillary Dale, Alex Hudgens, Christopher Mathew, Gayle Binney, Allie O'Neil, Alex Kostura, Sara Nitschke, Nigel Cooney, Christian Tanja, Seanna Petr, Debra Porter, Ho Kah Yoke, Sarah Havekost Hocine, Michelle Spatz, Thomas

Dargon, Jordan Cosby, Kim Brisse, Kate Williams, Scott Karrel, Chris Iverson, Tyler Thurston, Kevin Peterson, Clinton Ibarra, Skyler Jacobs, Marin Ping, Cassidy McDonald, Shane O'Neal, Frank Altman, Camila Ramirez-Arau, Danny Silk, Jessie Bullock, Aziza Moirabou, Stephanie O'Neal, Tyler Rhodes, Sara Perryman, Sally Bucey, Amy Goldman, Lauren Holroyd, Judith Wadness, Leslie Eldridge, Kelly McNulty, Jennica Bramble, Patty Hester, Tori Morris, Tyrone Shaw, Todd Langstaff, Tom Hernandez, Janine Feirer, Shannon Stevenson, Daniel Rabinowicz, Samhitha Raj, John Valgoi, Ellen Denis, Michelle Spangler Raddell, Bronwyn Williams, Kate Brolley, Monica Retka, Juan Vazquez, and Sylvie Do-Vu.

My knowledge of the hidden curriculum and the work of youth development organizations was largely derived from a series of interviews with so many dynamic folks working in this field. A huge thanks to you all: Kathleen Fuchs Hritz, Danielle Bolling, Mike Odiotti, Peter Raucci, Leovanny Fernandez, Chelsea Williams, Oriana Seastone, Wagaye Johannes, Shawon Jackson, Mark Moselle, Susan Johnson, David Thai, Mery Arcila, Chandra Waring, Mamadou Sow, Walt Wolfram, Duong Tran, Andrew Lowrance, Myles Durkee, Alejandro Gonzalez, Ali Thomas, Mary Hemenway, Andrea Flores, Luz Chung, Jacqueline Guan, Flo Capinding, Sylvie Do-Vu, Sara Johnson, Charisse Williams, Devki Rana, Ally Levy, Erin Mann, Nicole Petraglia, Ray Reyes, and Nancy Fairbank. My appreciation to those YDOs who were able to provide me access to numerous members of your team: Nate Pietrini, Karen Thomas, Benjamin Serrano, Alexa Ramirez, Jessica Mora at High Jump; Jordan Harrison, Dagim Aboye, Jessie Hernandez-Reyes at

Reality Changers; Benjamin Bingman-Tennant and Yasmine Jaffier-Williams at A Better Chance; Grace Bianciardi, Lena Eberhart, and Monica Duque at Let's Get Ready; Hetal Jani, Nafisha Noashin Sarker, Tatiana Nechaeva at SPEAK Mentorship; and David Thai, Mamadou Sow Duong Tran, Andrew Lowrance at Rise First.

On the meandering path to this point, many people have formatively influenced me. But I must acknowledge the folks who instilled my love of writing and helped hone my craft—my middle school language arts teacher, Debra Porter; my high school English teacher, Ashley Anderton; and my mentor, Sarah Havekost-Hocine.

One person has served in all the aforementioned roles and then some. To my love, Chris Caines. You encouraged me to pursue this crazy idea from the start, you insisted I would rock it in my moments of doubt, you listened to my brainstorms, you read every draft, you gave me frank feedback, and, most importantly, you kept me grounded in my hope that writing this book would be fun and energizing, not stressful. It's no surprise you've done all of this because you always go above and beyond for me, every day. I love you and appreciate you to no end.

Just as this book started, I must end it by thanking my parents. Your hustle, humility, and humor got me here. Like so many of the things we've done as a family, I could have never predicted I'd write a book. But you modeled that risk-taking and a sense of adventure can take you far. Thank you for everything you've done and continue to do for me. I love you.

Annex: YDOs At-A-Glance

YDO's At-A-Glance

YDO Name	Location	YDO Category	Highlights of Approach
Reality Changers	San Diego	College Prep & Skills Development	After-school program for low performing high school students to build academic skills and get college application support
Vocal Justice	Nationwide	Academic Enrichment	Trains teachers in critical consciousness and liberatory pedagogy to build students' communications and critical analysis skills
High Jump	Chicago	Academic Enrichment	After-school and summer program for high-achieving middle schoolers to be competitive for independent high schools
A Better Chance	Nationwide	Academic Placement	Works with middle school students on independent school placement and skills development
OneGoal	Nationwide	College Prep & Skills Development	Three-year program embedded within high schools for college prep and success
Let's Get Ready	Northeast	College Prep & Skills Development	Peer mentor and nudge model focused on academic enrichment, college preparedness and college application processes

YDO Name	Location	YDO Category	Highlights of Approach
SEO	New York and San Francisco	Academic Enrichment	Eight-year program in high school and college to build skills, college applications, and resilience to graduate through training and mentorship
Posse	Nationwide	Academic Placement	Identifies youth from urban cores for college placement opportunities
Prep for Prep	New York City	Academic Placement	Enrichment and placement program that identifies talented middle schoolers and places them in independent schools
Rise First	Nationwide	College Prep & Skills Development	First-gen student-led organization with mentoring and resource sharing
Oliver Scholars	New York City	Academic Placement	Supports middle school students to be placed in the most competitive schools in NYC and offers supplemental support throughout their studies

Bibliography

INTRODUCTION

- Barnum, Matt. "To and through: What research says about what works (and what doesn't) to help students complete college." Chalkbeat. January 15, 2020. https://www.chalkbeat.org/2020/1/15/21121860/to-and-through-what-research-says-about-what-works-and-what-doesn-t-to-help-students-complete-colleg

- Carnevale, Anthony P. and Jeff Strohl, "How Increasing College Access Is Increasing Inequality and What to Do about It," Rewarding Strivers: Helping Low-Income Students Succeed in College, ed. Richard D. Kahlenberg (New York: Century Foundation Press, 2020), 71-190, quoted in Anthony Abraham Jack. The Privileged Poor. Cambridge, MA: Harvard University Press, 2019. Kindle.

- Chetty, Raj. et al., "Mobility Report Cards: The Role of Colleges in Intergenerational Mobility" (Equality of Opportunity Project, NBER Working Paper no. 23618, revised, July 2017), quoted in Anthony Abraham Jack. The Privileged Poor. Cambridge, MA: Harvard University Press, 2019. Kindle.

- Jack, Anthony. *The Privileged Poor: How Elite Colleges are Failing Disadvantaged Students.* Boston, MA. Harvard University Press, 2019. Kindle.

- National Science Foundation, National Center for Science and Engineering Statistics. 2018. Doctorate Recipients from US Universities: 2017. Special Report NSF 19-301. Alexandria, VA. https://ncses.nsf.gov/pubs/nsf19301/.

- The Opportunity Network. "Our Work and the College and Career Landscape." Accessed June 15, 2021. https://opportunitynetwork.org/

- Waring, Chandra "Black and Biracial Americans Wouldn't Need to Code-switch If We Lived in a Post-racial Society." The Conversation. August 17, 2018. https://theconversation.com/black-and-biracial-americans-wouldnt-need-to-code-switch-if-we-lived-in-a-post-racial-society-101013

CHAPTER 1

- American Psychological Association. "Stereotype Threat Widens Achievement Gap." July 15, 2006. https://www.apa.org/research/action/stereotype

- Bourdieu, Pierre. "Cultural Reproduction and Social Reproduction." Studies in the Learning Sciences. Paris, France. 1975. http://piggottsclass.weebly.com/uploads/2/3/1/7/23179512/bourdieup_cultural_and_social_reproduction.pdf

- Chatelain, Marcia. "We Must Help First-Generation Students Master Academe's 'Hidden Curriculum'" The Chronicle of Higher Education. October 21, 2018. https://www.chronicle.com/article/we-must-help-first-generation-students-master-academes-hidden-curriculum/?cid=gen_sign_in

- Cole, Nicki Lisa. "What Is Cultural Capital? Do I Have It? An Overview of the Concept." ThoughtCo. September 23, 2019. https://www.thoughtco.com/what-is-cultural-capital-do-i-have-it-3026374

- Hobbes, Michael and Sarah Marshall. "The 'Ebonics' Controversy". *You're Wrong About*. Podcast. April 2019.

- Jack, Anthony. *The Privileged Poor: How Elite Colleges are Failing Disadvantaged Students.* Boston, MA. Harvard University Press, 2019. Kindle.

- McCluney, Courtney L., Kathrina Robotham, Serenity Lee, Richard Smith, and Myles Durkee. "The Costs of Code Switching." Harvard Business Review. November 15, 2019. https://hbr.org/2019/11/the-costs-of-codeswitching

- Sherald, Jalen. "The Buzz: Dear White People (and Everyone Else), Let's Talk About Code Switching" The Inclusion Solution. August 2, 2018. http://www.theinclusionsolution.me/buzz-buzz-dear-white-people-everyone-else-lets-talk-code-switching/

- Wolfram, Walt. "Everyone Has an Accent." Learning for Justice. Issue 18, Fall 2000.

- Wolfram, Walt. "Sound Effects: How to Challenge Language Prejudice in the Classroom." Learning for Justice. Issue 43, Spring 2013. https://www.learningforjustice.org/magazine/spring-2013/sound-effects

CHAPTER 2

- A Better Chance. "Mission and History" Accessed May 20, 2021. https://www.abetterchance.org/about/mission-history

- Jack, Anthony. *The Privileged Poor: How Elite Colleges are Failing Disadvantaged Students.* Boston, MA. Harvard University Press, 2019. Kindle.

- Let's Get Ready. "Program Model." Accessed June 25, 2021. https://letsgetready.org/program-model/

- Oliver Scholars. "Mission and History." Accessed June 25, 2021. https://www.oliverscholars.org/mission/

- Posse. "Mission & History." Accessed May 20, 2021. https://www.possefoundation.org/shaping-the-future/mission-history

- Reality Changers. "Our Story" Accessed May 20, 2021. https://realitychangers.org/our-story/

- SEO. "History." Accessed May 20, 2021. https://www.seo-usa.org/about-us/history/

- Year Up. "About." Accessed May 20, 2021. https://www.yearup.org/about

- YMCA. "History: 2000 to Present." Accessed May 20, 2021. https://www.ymca.net/history/2000-present.html

PART 2
- Rise First. "College Success Roadmap." Accessed May 19, 2021. https://risefirst.org/resources/success-roadmap

CHAPTER 3
- High Jump. "Program." Accessed May 19, 2021. https://highjumpchicago.org/program-overview

CHAPTER 4
- American Psychological Association. "Stereotype Threat Widens Achievement Gap." July 15, 2006. https://www.apa.org/research/action/stereotype

- Barnum, Matt. "More Than a Nudge: To Get More Students to and through College, Intensive Advising May Be Key." Chalkbeat.org (http://chalkbeat.org/), January 26, 2021.

- Friess, Steve. "Rural Students Often Go Unnoticed By Colleges. Can Virtual Counseling Put Them on the Map?" The Hechinger Report, June 11, 2019.

- Form Your Future. "FAFSA Tracker." Accessed May 19, 2021. https://formyourfuture.org/fafsa-tracker/

- Gates Foundation. "Navigating Financial Aid: Four Student Stories." April 30, 2018. 4:27. https://www.youtube.com/watch?v=wfQ74vakHLc

- Glass, Ira and Paul Tough. "The Campus Tour Has Been Cancelled." This American Life. Podcast. March 19, 2021. https://www.thisamericanlife.org/734/the-campus-tour-has-been-cancelled

- Jack, Anthony Abraham. "A Separate and Unequal System of College Admissions." The New York Times. September 16, 2020. https://www.nytimes.com/2020/09/15/books/review/selingo-korn-levitz-college-admissions.html

- Johnston, Andy. "One Surprising Barrier to College Success: Dense Higher Education Lingo" The Hechinger Report, June 14, 2019. https://hechingerreport.org/one-surprising-barrier-to-success-in-college-understanding-higher-education-lingo/

- Morton, Jennifer. *Moving Up Without Losing Your Way: The Ethical Costs of Upward Mobility.* Princeton. Princeton University Press, 2019.

- OneGoal. "OneGoal Fellows Share Their Experience in Listen & Learn Event." February 26, 2021. 55:12. https://www.youtube.com/watch?v=m6L_1B-q6Gg

- Tough, Paul. *The Inequality Machine: How College Divides Us.* New York, NY. Houghton Mifflin Harcourt, 2019.

- U.S. News and World Report. "Williams College." Accessed May 19, 2021. https://www.usnews.com/best-colleges/williams-college-2229

CHAPTER 5

- Gable, Rachel. *The Hidden Curriculum: First Generation Students at Legacy Universities.* Princeton, NJ. Princeton University Press, 2021.

- Jack, Anthony. *The Privileged Poor: How Elite Colleges are Failing Disadvantaged Students.* Boston, MA. Harvard University Press, 2019. Kindle.

- University of Georgia. "1st At the First: A Handbook for First-In-The-Family Students at UGA"." Accessed May 19, 2021. http://firstgen.uga.edu/firstgenhandbookstudentresize.pdf

CHAPTER 6

- Chatelain, Marcia. "We Must Help First-Generation Students Master Academe's 'Hidden Curriculum.'" The Chronicle of Higher Education. October 21, 2018. https://www.chronicle.com/article/we-must-help-first-generation-students-master-academes-hidden-curriculum/?cid=gen_sign_in

- Crucet, Jennine Capo. "Taking My Parents To College." The New York Times. August 22, 2015. https://www.nytimes.com/2015/08/23/opinion/sunday/taking-my-parents-to-college.html

- Gable, Rachel. *The Hidden Curriculum: First Generation Students at Legacy Universities*. Princeton, NJ. Princeton University Press, 2021.

- Grad Bag. "Our Work". Accessed June 22, 2021. http://www.gradbag.org/our-work-2

- Jack, Anthony. *The Privileged Poor: How Elite Colleges are Failing Disadvantaged Students*. Boston, MA. Harvard University Press, 2019. Kindle.

- Johnston, Andy. "One Surprising Barrier to College Success: Dense Higher Education Lingo" The Hechinger Report, June 14, 2019. https://hechingerreport.org/one-surprising-barrier-to-success-in-college-understanding-higher-education-lingo/

CHAPTER 7

- DiversityAbroad. "2019-2023 Strategic Plan: Diversity Abroad Forward." 2019. https://cdn.ymaws.com/www.diversitynetwork.org/resource/resmgr/2019_diversityabroad_forward.pdf

- Gable, Rachel. *The Hidden Curriculum: First Generation Students at Legacy Universities*. Princeton, NJ. Princeton University Press, 2021.

- Kuh, George D. Association of American Colleges and Universities. "High-Impact Educational Practices." Accessed May 19, 2021. https://www.aacu.org/node/4084

- Llewellyn, Brittany M. "Race and the Ivy." The Harvard Crimson. June 1, 2008. https://www.thecrimson.com/article/2008/6/1/race-and-the-ivy-as-400/

- National Association of Colleges and Employers. "Minority College Students Underrepresented in Paid Internships." September 9, 2020. https://www.naceweb.org/about-us/press/minority-college-students-underrepresented-in-paid-internships/?utm_source=linkedin&utm_medium=social&utm_content=post&utm_campaign=content

- Tomkiw, Lydia. "2010 Marks 40 Years of Coeducation." The Wesleyan Argus. March 25, 2010. http://wesleyanargus.com/2010/03/25/2010-marks-40-years-of-coeducation/

CHAPTER 8
- Morton, Jennifer. *Moving Up Without Losing Your Way: The Ethical Costs of Upward Mobility*. Princeton. Princeton University Press, 2019.

CHAPTER 9
- El-Amin, Aaliyah. "Until Justice Rolls Down Like Water: Revisiting Emancipatory Schooling for African Americans – A Theoretical Exploration of Concepts for Liberation." PhD dissertation. Harvard University, 2015.

CHAPTER 10

- Ladson-Billings, Gloria. "Culturally Relevant Pedagogy 2.0: a.k.a. the Remix" Harvard Educational Review. Vol 84. No 1 (Spring 2014). pg 74 https://www.proquest.com/docview/1511014412

- Seider, Scott, Aaliyah El-Amin, and Lauren Leigh Kelly. "The Development of Critical Consciousness." In L. Arnett Jensen (Ed.), Oxford Handbook of Moral Development: An Interdisciplinary Perspective. Oxford University Press (2020) pg. 360-385.

CHAPTER 11

- Cunningham, Victor. "Prep for Prep and the Fault Lines in New York's Schools" The New Yorker, March 2020. https://www.newyorker.com/magazine/2020/03/09/prep-for-prep-and-the-fault-lines-in-new-yorks-schools

- Jack, Anthony. *The Privileged Poor: How Elite Colleges are Failing Disadvantaged Students.* Boston, MA. Harvard University Press, 2019. Kindle.

- Morton, Jennifer. *Moving Up Without Losing Your Way: The Ethical Costs of Upward Mobility.* Princeton. Princeton University Press, 2019.

CHAPTER 12

- Chang, Alvin. "The Subtle Ways Colleges Discriminate against Poor Students, Explained with a Cartoon." Vox. September

12, 2018. https://www.vox.com/2017/9/11/16270316/college-mobility-culture

- Morton, Jennifer. *Moving Up Without Losing Your Way: The Ethical Costs of Upward Mobility.* Princeton. Princeton University Press, 2019.

CHAPTER 13

- "Black at Exeter" Instagram account. Accessed June 10, 2021. https://www.instagram.com/blackatexeter/?hl=en

- Cunningham, Victor. "Prep for Prep and the Fault Lines in New York's Schools" The New Yorker, March 2020. https://www.newyorker.com/magazine/2020/03/09/prep-for-prep-and-the-fault-lines-in-new-yorks-schools

- DegreesNYC. "Our Approach." Accessed June 10, 2021. https://degreesnyc.wordpress.com/about/

- Edelman, Peter. "Foreward." in The Youth Development Handbook: Coming of Age in American Communities. Edited by Stephen F. and Mary Agnes Hamilton. Pages vii-viii. Thousand Oaks, CA. 2004.

- National Association for College Admissions Counseling. "Association Overview." Accessed June 10, 2021 https://www.nacacnet.org/about/overview/

- National College Attainment Network. "Home Page" Accessed June 10, 2021. https://www.ncan.org/

- Student Success Network. "Improvement Lab." Accessed June 10, 2021. https://www.studentsuccessnetwork.org/improvement-lab

- Swaak, Taylor. "Within NYC's Highly Segregated School System, a Group of Low-Income Students Sacrifice Their Summers, Weekends for a Chance at College Success." The 74, February 11, 2020. https://www.the74million.org/article/within-nycs-highly-segregated-school-system-a-group-of-low-income-students-sacrifice-their-summers-weekends-for-a-chance-at-college-success/

- Youth Development Institute. "Home Page" Accessed June 10, 2021. https://www.ydinstitute.org/

- Young Invincibles. "Home Page" Accessed June 10, 2021. https://younginvincibles.org/

www.ingramcontent.com/pod-product-compliance
Lightning Source LLC
LaVergne TN
LVHW012100070526
838200LV00074BA/3826